Not Enc
My fath

One man's survival in captivity in the Far East during
WWII

**"I will recover and remember
I will never forget"**

DUKE SELL

**Foreword by
Major General Sir William Cubitt KCVO CBE DL**

Chiselbury

I dedicate this book to all my family
To the grandchildren, and the great-grandchildren that my father
never got to meet
May his memory live on through you all

And to all FEPOWs. May you never, ever, be forgotten

Contents

Acknowledgements

My nephew, Mark Sell, my father's eldest grandson, who's invaluable assistance helped me put this book together.

Jacqueline Jeynes, who has done a marvellous job editing the book.

C.O.F.E.P.O.W. Children and families of the Far East Prisoners of War

VJ Day

The Far Eastern FEPOWS Wall of Heroes

Descendants of Thai-Burma Railway WW2 POWs

WW2 Burma Research

Memories of the Norfolk, Royal Norfolk and Royal Anglian Regiments

The Royal Norfolk Regiment Living History Group

T.B.R.C.

Thai-Burma Railway Centre "Death Railway Museum", Kanchanaburi, Thailand

Keith Andrews, who helped me with my research.

Malcolm Windsor and Andy Curtis, for both reviewing my book.

To my beautiful wife, Lynne, for putting up with all of my emotions writing this book.

I thank you all.

The details included here are based on my father's memories, so reflect his feelings about the events and the people he met along the way. It is also based on reflections and recollections of his friends from that time, and historical facts from a range of reference sources in the public domain.

Any controversial comments or any factual errors throughout this book are mine, mine alone, and are not my father's words.

Foreword by
Major General Sir William Cubitt KCVO CBE DL

This book adds to the record of the 60,000 allied troops who were captured by the Imperial Japanese Army in February 1942 and were taken to Thailand to construct a railway, under extreme duress, from Thailand to Burma by which the Japanese forces would supply their ill-fated campaign in Burma. The prisoners of war faced exceptional hardship from the harsh conditions, disease and from their captors. One in five of the 30,000 British soldiers who worked on that railway died. One who endured some of the worst episodes but survived was Colour Sergeant Johnnie Sell of the 4th Battalion Royal Norfolk Regiment. This book tells his story. It has been written by his son, Duke Sell, long after his father's death in 1979, from memories of what he had been told and from records that he and others have researched.

The book tells the story of a tough soldier – a boxer – who faced extreme hardship with courage and survived, though affected by his experiences for life. He suffered personally from brutality, appalling conditions and ill-health. It is an extraordinary story of resilience under the most extreme of circumstances.

My own father was there too, in the 5th Norfolks, and his story followed a similar path. I visited the sites in 2019 assisted by the wonderful Thailand-Burma Railway Centre in Kanchanaburi that has done so much to research and record the detail of what happened, where and to whom. My father recorded the worst period as being in mid-1943 when the Imperial Japanese Army was desperate to complete the railway and forced even those clearly unable to work to return to the work parties. The POWs had marched up-country for days, already seriously degraded in their physical condition through exertion and lack of food, when they were hit by an early and heavy monsoon season and waves of cholera that swept through the camps killing thousands. It must have been hell on earth.

The book brings out many of the aspects that have been covered by earlier books such as the frustration at being surrendered without too much of a fight, the appalling conditions of the long train journey from Singapore to Thailand, the harshness of being slave labourers under cruel guards, instances of brutality, long marches through the jungle, improvised clothing, the impact of dysentery and cholera on already sick men and the appalling loss of life. It also tells some of the more positive aspects such as the brave support of local Thai people and the amazing performance of allied medical staff, themselves prisoners, who performed miracles without medical supplies and under extremely austere conditions. Colour Sergeant Sell was operated on for a burst duodenal ulcer in a POW makeshift hospital. There are even occasional glimpses of good humour of the POWs in the darkness.

No one could be expected to come through all this without enduring physical and mental scars and yet the FEPOWs bore these with courage after the war for the rest of their lives. For many, including Colour Sergeant Sell, a sense of anger and betrayal remained with them for the rest of their lives: anger at their treatment by the Imperial Japanese Army during the war, a feeling of having been

4

forgotten by their own side not only in captivity but also for decades after the recovery of the POWs to the UK, anger at the lenient treatment of many Japanese and Korean guards by the war crimes courts after the war, a hatred of all-things Japanese, outrage at the State Visit granted to the wartime Emperor Hirohito in 1971, and scorn at paltry compensation in 2000.

The author adds description of some other aspects of the Japanese campaigns in the Far East, including medical experiments on prisoners, the provision of forced 'comfort women' to their troops and biological warfare research.

The book concludes with two moving aspects. The first is the astonishingly strong and emotional bond that existed between survivors after the war, as witnessed by the author when he accompanied his father on a tour of old comrades in Norfolk. The second is the touching description of Admiral of the Fleet Lord Mountbatten's visit to the Sell household on the Isle of Wight in 1978 recalling the moment when Colour Sergeant Sell had been in a parade of POWs for him in Rangoon after their release in 1945.

It is worth reflecting that, mercifully, time has moved on and the modern Japan is a respected ally. Indeed, I led a British Army delegation to Japan in the early 2000s which I realise some former FEPOWs would have found hard to comprehend.

The author stresses that he has written about a man – his father – whom he held in awe, in order to ensure that the story of the suffering of the Far East Prisoners of War continues to be recognised. He has done him proud and I am privileged to have been asked to write a Foreword to this powerful book about a remarkable man.

Introduction

This is the story of my father, Johnnie Sell.

I asked him on several occasions, "Dad, why don't you write a book about your experiences, the world really needs to know?" His response was plain and simple, as it often was.

"Son, there's been enough written but not enough said."

Not enough said. Fair point.

However, I know he did not put pen to paper because he was afraid to re-live the myriad painful experiences he had been forced to endure. He suffered. A lot. That was one of the main reasons he, and other prisoners like him, did not write memoirs once they came home, but remember they were all told (by the government of the day) not to publicly state what had happened to them as Prisoners of War (POWs).

So, I am doing it. I want to. I need to. And you need to know.

I have read many books about the horrors Far East Prisoners of War (FEPOWs) endured, from all ranks of military personnel. Low ranking and high, they all detail their experiences of total horror and their will to survive despite the odds.

My book is not solely about the military journey of an Englishman enduring the horrors of war, it is the story of how I came to respect the greatest man I ever knew. Inevitably, I cannot avoid detailing the shocking treatment our troops were made to suffer as I too want the world to know what they went through. But this is a personal journey, a story of the love and respect I had for my father as I listened, wide-eyed, to his perspective on war and suffering and how the love for his family would see him through the darkest of times.

As you can see, I am filled with immense pride for my father, my family and all its achievements, and of the Norfolk Regiment itself.

My Father's Story

1: **Dad**

My father, Johnnie Sell, joined up in London on August 17th 1929, much to my grandmother's dismay.

"Why would you want to enlist in the army? To follow in your father's footsteps?", she asked.

He would often tell us how much he adored his father. Why the Norfolks? I didn't know that my grandfather was originally from Suffolk and had moved to London, to the 'Big Smoke', to find work. My Grandfather, John Sell, served with the Norfolks during World War I. Dad followed suit and joined, "fiddling" his age, to become a regular soldier with the 1st Battalion Norfolk Regiment. This regiment later became the Royal Norfolks in 1935. When my eldest brother, Terry, was called up for National Service in the 1950s, there was only one regiment in which he was going to serve.

Corporal Terence Sell served right up until the amalgamation of the Norfolks and Suffolks, becoming the Royal East Anglian Regiment. Three generations of the Sell family in the Norfolks then. So, the Norfolk Regiment and the county of Norfolk itself will always hold a special place in my heart.

Dad had enlisted and was now off to the Britannia Barracks, Norwich, for his introduction and basic training in the army - 1 year and 193 days - before being shipped off to India.

Dad (on the right) on his enlistment 1929

The only place I know where my father was stationed is Jhansi, an historic city in the Indian State of Utter Pradesh. He served alongside the Gurkha Regiment at Jhansi and told me these guys were the best fighting force he had ever seen. After the war, Dad was presented with a large Gurkha knife shaped like a boomerang - a kukri - and two smaller ones. He was immensely proud of these and once told me that when a knife has been drawn by a Gurkha, there will be blood!

It wasn't long before, under an Indian sky, he began earning his stripes to become Full Corporal and a keen member of the Regimental Boxing Team, this was in addition to being the captain of the football team and member of the hockey team - quite the sportsman.

My Dad, captain of the Regimental football team, quite the sportsman

My father the boxer

His boxing career was an important part of his life so deserves a special mention.

Just by chance, as research for this book, I wrote to the Royal East Anglian Regiment to ask if there were any records of Dad's boxing career whilst serving with the Norfolks in India. To my surprise, a large official looking envelope arrived a few weeks later detailing all my father's fights round by round. In the ring he had acquired the nickname 'Gentleman John'.

As a child, I recall answering the door to a somewhat irate man demanding he speak to my father. When Dad came to the door, the man was screaming and shouting about my brother picking flowers from his garden and, as some form of retribution, wanted to fight my father. As usual, Dad was as cool as a cucumber. With pride, I recall him asking the man if that was what he really wanted or would he prefer him to pay for the flowers and forget the whole thing.

Mr. Irate would not accept the offer, he wanted to fight. So, my father reluctantly said, "OK old boy, put 'em up."

With that, the man, delighted that he had got what he came for and with a smile on his face, threw the first punch. Dad blocked it masterfully, speedily followed by a ferocious uppercut and a 'swift one two'. It was all over. Picking himself up off the road, the wounded man hastily retreated to his house and his beloved garden. He should have taken the money for the flowers. Gentleman John indeed.

He taught me to box as a boy and as a young man - I still could not get close to him, even remotely. You would think that being in the ring, a fighter, would have made him

14

irascible, but in all our years together, I never once saw him lose his temper. He would say,

"Lose your temper in the ring and you lose the fight - the same applies outside of the ring." Dad was man of few words, but they often struck a chord.

Another wise saying he instilled in me, which has stayed with me throughout my life, are sage words which I intend to pass on to my grandchildren:

"A man's not a man who can throw a punch; a man's a man who can take one."

He also told me that if you know you are right, then fight your corner. Don't give in to anyone or anything. If you lose, it doesn't make you any less of a man.

In Rawalpindi, Dad had his first fight (1934) in the Inter-Company Novices Boxing Competition where he fought and won against Private Waterton. The Open Boxing Competition was held the following week and entries were limited to two per weight per company and only winners and runners up from the Novices were allowed to compete. Dad was now officially part of the regiment's welter weight boxing team.

There are some fascinating entries in the records of the time.

Norfolk Regiment vs Welch Regiment

Lance-Corporal Sell (Norfolks) beat Private Rees on points. Rees scored chiefly with swings in the opening round but was content to let Sell force the fight and rely on his left. The last round found Sell using straight blows against Rees' swinging and the former snatched a narrow points decision in a very close fight.

Lance-Corporal Sell (Norfolks) beat Private Rooke on points. Sell found it difficult to counter Rooke's tearaway methods at the start but once he stood off and boxed his opponent, instead of attempting to mix it, he forged ahead and was a good winner.

The final of the Eastern Command Boxing Competition, and with it the right to enter the semifinals of the Army team championships, was fought between 1st Battalion Norfolk Regiment and 1st Battalion The Cameronians at Jhansi in 1935. As you can see, it was not all easy going for Dad, but he won in the end.

Welter Weight Lance-Corporal Sell v Lance-Corporal Skinners. Skinners' heavy punch was evident from the commencement, Sell being 'dropped' three times in the first round. The Norfolk man boxed cleverly in the next round, to gain the lead with several good lefts to the face. The deciding round was all in favour of Sell who won the fight.

My father, Regimental boxing champion, India

The Norfolk Regiment vs 1st Royal Dragoons

Although the Regiment won by nine fights to two, there were many good contests. Lance-Corporal Sell, a newcomer to the team since last year, did exceedingly well to fight back as he did in the second and third rounds after a very severe first round against him. So well did he box, that it was a very close thing at the end of the third round. Another win for Sell.

The Norfolk Regiment went on to become All India Boxing Champions beating the holders, The 1st Battalion, The Kings Shropshire Light Infantry and the Royals, then The Cameronians, 2nd Battalion The Welch Regiment, and The Somersets.

Dad never lost a bout for the regiment. This was to stand him in good stead later when he became a prisoner of the Japanese.

The regimental boxing team. My father 2nd row, 3rd from left

18

Leaving India

Dad's spell of duty in India was drawing to a close. The last photograph taken there shows the Land of the Five Rivers Lodge in Jhansi. This is the Buffaloes' (The Royal Antediluvian Order of Buffaloes) equivalent to the

Free Masons - The RAOB is one of the largest fraternal organisations in the United Kingdom. The order started in 1822 and is known as the *Buffs* (not to be confused with the infantry battalion of the same name) to members. In this photograph there are a few guys that went on to become FEPOWs with my father, and others that fought the Japanese throughout India and Burma.

19

Whilst in India he became accustomed to the weather conditions - often too hot and too humid - and his skin became like leather. On his return from India, after serving 6 years and 8 months in total, his final assessments of conduct and character on leaving the Colours read as follows:

Military conduct: Exemplary. Testimonial: Honest, sober, reliable, keen and trustworthy. A good and keen sportsman. Has always done well. Has intelligence and common sense. A good man who should do very well in the future. Is strongly recommended. Signed by Lieutenant-Colonel Commanding 1st Battalion The Royal Norfolks. Transferred to the Army Reserve.

He served for just over six years in India and mentioned often, perhaps unfairly, that the women were beautiful but the men untrustworthy. This comment regarding trust, or lack of it, with regard to Indian men seemed a little 'off the cuff' and prejudiced but was later to prove prophetic at the fall of Singapore.

2: Preparation for war in the Far East

When Dad returned from India in March 1937, he was a Full Corporal and was immediately placed in the reserves. He got a job in a local hospital, St Giles Hospital, Camberwell as a porter, which is where he met my mother, Irene, also from Camberwell. In September of the next year my brother Terry was born.

To subsidise his very poor income from the hospital, every Friday night after work he would attend the ring. This is where his boxing background as Regimental boxing champion would stand him in good stead. Known locally as Blackfriars Ring in Southwark, South-East London, he would fight boxers of his own weight – known today as "prize-fighting".

The winner of each fight would receive the princely sum of 7/6d (35p in modern money). This prize money would cover the cost of their rent. But it would be supplemented according to how well you performed in the ring – both putting on a very good fight and winning. Showing their appreciation, the audience would throw coins into the ring. There wasn't one Friday night where my father didn't bring home a hat full of money.

He was a man's man. He once told me there will be times in your life when you just want men's company. It wasn't until I got much older that I knew what he meant.

World War II was just around the corner and Singapore, an island of gentle hills and ridges, 27 miles long by 13 miles wide, was under scrutiny. It was considered to be the jewel in the crown of the British Empire, some said an impregnable fortress. By 1936, British strategists believed any attack on Singapore would come by sea. However, British Army Intelligence Officer, Joe Vinden, believed otherwise. He thought if Singapore were to be invaded, a land invasion via Malaya would be more logical. He even predicted, after surveying Singapore, Korta Bharu as a perfect landing place for an invasion.

His advice to the British government that money should be spent on new aircraft, instead of the ongoing fortification of Singapore, was ignored. Singapore's 15 inch naval guns were mostly facing the wrong way and, indeed, had been supplied with armour-piercing ammunition intended for use against ships. Against men they were almost useless.

It is not clear whether anyone actually read the report sent in by Joe Vinden, but the fault for that appeared to lay with Lieutenant-General Arthur Percival. It is not appropriate to allocate blame in these circumstances as statements at the time (from various official records/sources) suggest many senior politicians and military personnel misread the situation.

Dad was recalled to the reserves of the 4th Battalion Royal Norfolks on December 1st 1939. The Battalion, under the command of Lieutenant-Colonel JH Jewson MC TD (whom my father held in high regard, declaring him a fine officer), was based in Norwich. The early weeks of the war were spent in providing guards on vulnerable points and aerodromes, with some training carried out under these difficult and scattered conditions. A move to Gorleston holiday camp brought the Battalion together as a unit in

Yarmouth. This move greatly simplified training, which had now begun in earnest, a draft of NCOs and other ranks proving to be a great help in assisting the training.

The personnel who were drafted in included:
- CSM Lunn, who later became RSM (Regimental Sergeant Major) and was killed in action in Singapore.
- Corporal FE Brown, later to become RSM
- W Nelson, a CSM (Company Sergeant Major)
- Sell, a CQMS (Company Quartermaster Sergeant).
- Second-in-command was Major AE Knights MC MM.

A and D companies were stationed at Yarmouth. The Battalion was brigaded with the 4th and 5th Battalions of the Suffolk Regiment to form 54 Infantry Brigade under Brigadier EHW Backhouse [as part of the 18th Infantry Division].

In July 1940, the Battalion received its first intake of men enlisted under the Conscription Act. Plans for the training had been carefully prepared and Captain WL Faux and CSM Rice were entrusted with this interesting and responsible work. The results were extraordinarily good. Dad served with CSM Rice in India and they were very good friends, although CSM Rice (who also had a brother) died in captivity. I always remember my father referring to one of the brothers as Tuppenny Rice.

I do not know when Dad became Colour Sergeant but between 1939/41 he, along with a mate who was also a boxer in the regimental boxing team, were sent on a training course in Plymouth. The Royal Marines based in Plymouth thought that the insignia (Britannia) badge should have been theirs. Knowing this detail whilst on a night out in town, and aware of the Marines' covetousness of the badge, Dad and his friend decided to protect themselves. By this I mean both had knuckledusters in their pockets and it wasn't long before they were put to use.

It was their last night in Plymouth when they ventured out for a drink. Dad said that they picked a backstreet pub away from where the Marines frequented. It wasn't long after they ordered their first drink that eight Marines walked in, all Privates. They soon spotted the Britannia worn by two NCOs of the Norfolk Regiment at the end of the bar. Initially, light-hearted banter flowed between the men, largely directed from the Marines to the Norfolks. But the situation soon turned nasty as the Marines approached the Norfolks demanding they take off their badges and hand them over to them. No member of any regiment would ever dream of handing anything over that belonged to them and their regiment; it was a matter of honour. My father told me he turned to his mate and nodded to him to signify dusters on and let's finish this. The Marines never got the Britannia, they got a beating. They couldn't have picked on the two worse men to tussle with if they had tried.

While training was in full flow in Yarmouth, my father decided to rent a house in Gorleston so that my mother and brother could come up from London to be closer to him.

By 1940 quite a lot of the men were getting twitchy, asking when it would be their turn, training completed. When was the 18th Division going to be involved in the war?

They didn't have long to wait.

When word got out that King George VI was to inspect the Battalion at Gorleston there was an air of excitement among the men. It was believed the Battalion would soon go abroad. The 18th Division was indeed on the move, initially to Cambridge for more specialised training, and for nearly 3 weeks all ranks were hard at work, with frequent specialist courses to bring variety to the reparation. Gradually the 4th Battalion was taking shape and settling down into an efficient and well-trained unit. Shortly before Christmas, the 18th Division received orders to proceed overseas to Egypt to complete its training.

They were ordered to Scotland and on January 8th 1941, 54th Brigade was concentrated near Hawick. Dad said the first few weeks were intensely cold, 38° of frost being recorded on January 18th and deep snow lying on the hillsides. This lasted until well into February and interfered considerably with training, although it served an excellent purpose in toughening up the Battalion and brought opportunities for skiing. During March, brigade and divisional schemes were carried out to exercise the movements of troops, to test marching powers, and to practice the seizing and holding of bridgehead positions. It was all very serious.

On one occasion, the Battalion marched 22 miles in one day from Hawick to Melrose - but it was excellent training and by the time the next move came along, the whole Brigade was working together as a team. The decision to move 18th Division to Egypt to finish its training there was cancelled in the early part of 1941 - a change of plan that was to have far reaching effects on the Battalion when its turn came for action. These guys must have been sick to the back teeth, what with all the training and being no closer to seeing combat.

Instead of Egypt, 54th Brigade moved to Blackburn in mid-April under the command of Major General MB Beckwith-Smith. Divisional exercises were continued in the neighbourhood throughout May. In June, the Battalion underwent a two-day endurance test consisting of a route march, night operations, a scheme which included field firing and a final route march back to Blackburn. All ranks came through it well, earning the congratulations of the Divisional Commander and the Brigadier. From Blackburn, the Battalion moved on August 13th to Ross-on-Wye for the next stage of its training. This initially consisted of route marches with a return across country in the fastest possible time and, additionally, night operations. Later this also included river crossings in assault boats, both by day and night.

The Battalion, with other units in the division stationed in the vicinity of Ross-on-Wye, was inspected by an unwell His Majesty the King shortly before leaving the area. On this occasion Lieutenant-Colonel Knights was decorated by the King, receiving from him the Territorial Decoration. As Dad said, this was a unique honour (but thoroughly deserved by a hardened soldier) as His Majesty does not usually make a personal decoration of this nature.

During September, instructions were received by the Battalion to hold itself in readiness for operations overseas. Tropical kit was issued, vehicles prepared for shipment, and reinforcements received to replace men unfit for service abroad. The time had come for the 4th Battalion to leave Ross-on-Wye and go on to Liverpool.

"Ere we go lads, it's our turn." A sergeant cried out.

If only they knew where they were heading and what lay in store for them.

By this time, my mother and brother had returned to London, not knowing where my father was heading nor the long hard years that lay ahead for her and many like her. Clueless and oblivious to where their men were going, or for how long, was extraordinarily difficult for these young women, wives and girlfriends, some with children.

Hardly anything has been written about the heartache of the families left behind. My mother worked at Waterloo station in London during the war watching troops leaving for abroad. It was the ones that returned that really upset her - wounded men, some severely, some fatally. Every day was the same, always thinking about Dad. Was he alive? Was he well? Where, indeed, was he? It was a long time before my mother received news from the War Office stating that my father was in Japanese hands. I believe that all the families became part of the "forgotten".

On October 28th, most of the 18th Infantry Division proceeded to Liverpool where it embarked in a fleet of transports, the Battalion sailing in the *Andes*. The majority of these young men, who had hardly ever left their home county, now found themselves travelling up and down the country and were finally about to sail - the adrenaline must have been pumping in trepidation. Dad was quite used to all this travelling, having served in India for six and a half years with the 1st Battalion before the war. He also had the stomach for the high seas, whereas many others didn't and succumbed to seasickness.

The destination of the *Andes* was unknown, but there was a tremendous feeling of excitement and relief. At last, the long months of training were over and the future held many hopes. The convoy, heavily escorted by destroyers, sailed out into the Atlantic the next day. On November 2nd, midway between Great Britain and Canada, an American squadron, took over escort duties and they now knew that the first destination was Halifax, Nova Scotia. The *Andes* went alongside the battleship and aircraft carrier *Lexington*, and the Battalion transferred to the American transporter, *Wakefield*. Before her war service, she was a luxury ocean-liner but was now converted into a troop transporter equipped with hammocks for all the men. Dad was pleased to say the food was very good.

The voyage continued, the convoy now consisting of six American troopships escorted by aircraft carrier *Ranger*, two cruisers and eight destroyers. The final destination of the division was still unknown to the men. A month later, the convoy steamed into Cape Town.

By now, the Japanese attack on Pearl Harbour had taken place and the United States had entered the war. A cheer went up amongst the troops, not for the fact that Pearl Harbour had been bombed and many had lost their lives, no, the cheer was for the fact that they were not alone in this war anymore. Dad said that some even thought the war would soon be over with the Yanks alongside us. How wrong they were.

The Japanese had already landed in Malaya, but most of the troops were unaware of this, believing they were heading for Egypt. Three days were spent in Cape Town, giving all the ranks a chance to stretch their legs and enjoy the lavish hospitality of the local inhabitants. On December 13th, the convoy set off again, steaming up the East African coast past Madagascar and then out into the Indian Ocean.

Five days later, it was announced that the final destination for the 18th Division was Bombay, which they reached on December 27th. The Battalion disembarked the following day and moved by train, with the rest of the Brigade, to Ahmednagar for further training. This was carried out throughout the day, in excruciating heat, although Dad "was used to" these conditions having already endured the heat of India a few years earlier. However, conditions were arduous and once again, my father, Colour Sergeant Johnny Sell, was involved in the training.

His rank at this time is an important feature of Dad's service. In terms of rank, Colour Sergeant is above Sergeant and below Warrant Officer. It was at the request of the Duke of Wellington that the special rank of Colour Sergeant was instituted in 1813 for those whose duty it was to act as escort to the Colours. Apparently, he was greatly impressed by the bravery shown by Sergeants escorting the Colours so desired that they should have a special rank. Hence, they were, and still are, known as Colour

Sergeants. NCOs - Non-Commissioned Officers – are, and always have been, *'the backbone of the British Army; the driving force behind the men'*.

Going back to the situation they found themselves in at Ahmednagar, there were additional difficulties due to the fact that the Battalion's transport was in another ship and had not yet arrived. Furthermore, the Battalion was held in constant readiness for another move. Orders to proceed to Bombay came on January 11th 1942. Even though the destination was still a secret, few could doubt that this was the first step towards Malaya, where the Japanese had been advancing with alarming rapidity down the peninsular, and where the situation was already becoming critical.

On January 15th, they reached Bombay. Once again, 54th Brigade embarked on the *USS Wakefield*, with the remainder of the division in other ships. The convoy sailed at 13:00 hours on the 19th, its destination given as the Southwest Pacific Area. Pamphlets on jungle warfare were issued, and all ranks attempted to learn something about the new type of warfare that lay ahead for all our guys.

As the convoy passed through Banka Straits on January 28th, it was sighted by a Japanese aircraft which dropped six bombs, fortunately without result. That night, to avoid any bunching of the ships in narrow waters, the three fastest vessels were ordered ahead at full speed. The *USS Wakefield*, with Dad and the 54th Brigade onboard, won the race to Keppel Harbour in Singapore on the January 29th.

And so the story begins.

3: The battle for Singapore

Although the news from Malaya was not encouraging, spirits were high in the Battalion. They could not have known that within 17 days, all the months of hard work since 1939 would be wasted. Singapore would fall to the Japanese.

The battle for Singapore fell into two distinct phases. During the first, from January 29th to February 9th, there was little activity for the Battalion. 18th Infantry Division was responsible for the defence of the North Eastern sector of Singapore Island. At the time, the British called Singapore, somewhat disparagingly, the city of "chinks, drinks and stinks'. Most of its 750,000 Malay and Chinese inhabitants lived in squalor, yet they had faith that the British would protect them.

During this period of little activity, the men were warned about certain areas known for prostitution and to stay well clear because of the consequences of venereal diseases. When you have 90,000 or so men on an island, thousands of miles away from home, there were quite a few that took some 'comfort' believing they may be dead at any time anyway. Those that did catch a 'dose' would soon rue the day and wish they had listened to their superiors.

Their area stretched from Fairy Point near Changi on the right to Seletar Aerodrome on the left, extending as far south as the Tampines Road and Thompson Village, near MacRitchie Reservoirs. On disembarkation, the Battalion was taken by lorries to a tented camp on the Tampines Road. During the second night under canvas, the last British troops to escape from mainland Malaya made their way to the island over the causeway, across Johore Strait. The causeway was blown up behind them and Singapore Island, separated from the mainland, was hurriedly prepared for a last stand against the enemy.

Already the difficulties of defence were being recognised. The most obvious problem was the complete lack of fighter cover overhead, leaving the air space for Japanese bombers to make the most of the opportunity. This is where I, personally, am at a loss to understand why they sent an army intelligence officer, Joe Vinden, to Singapore before the war to survey the weakness of the island. He then sent back a report stating that money should be spent on aircraft, but this was completely ignored. Mystifying. In 1940, Sir Shenton Thomas, governor of the Straits Settlements in Singapore, put in a request for more aircraft to protect against any invading force. Again, this request was ignored. Who was held accountable for these mistakes? All we know is that nobody was.

There was a shortage of full equipment. Some of it was not landed from the transporters until February 8th, some had been lost in daily air attacks on the dock areas of Singapore, and another explanation was, apparently, due to the 'thinness' of allied troops on the ground. Singapore Island is roughly 27 miles long by 13 miles wide. Its' defenders consisted of 18th Division, 11th Indian Division, 53rd Infantry Brigade, and the remains of the Australian Division. None had been trained in jungle warfare except for a few of the Indian personnel and some of the Australians. At the end of January, Lieutenant-General

Arthur Percival released a press statement "under extreme duress and orders from Churchill". It read:

"The battle of Malaya has come to an end and the battle of Singapore has started. Our task is to hold this fortress until help can come, as surely it will come. This we are determined to do. In carrying out this task we want the help of every man and woman in the fortress. There is work for all to do. Any enemy who sets foot in our fortress must be dealt with immediately. The enemy within our gates must be ruthlessly weeded out. There must be no more loose talk and rumour-mongering. Our duty is clear. With firm resolve and fixed determination we shall win through."

The report was sent to every officer.

This statement was sent out about the same time as Churchill sent Percival a memo stating that Singapore must not fall.

"Every man and officer must defend to the last man." wrote Churchill.

For the first few days, the Battalion remained in brigade reserve to form a force for counter-attack should the Japanese attempt a landing in their area. Battalion HQ consisted of HQ company under Major RF Humphrey, and A Company under Captain M Gowing who were stationed in the Teck Hock area. B Company with Major WL Faux was about two miles from Teck Hock, C Company and Captain TC Eaton was in the Serangoon Jetty area, and D Company under Captain SF Phillips was in the Serangoon Church area.

The first phase of attack

One of the many discussions I had with my father was about the last few days leading up to the surrender of Singapore, when he was on reconnaissance in the Bukit Tamah area, and while the Battalion was in retreat. His driver, Flash, was shot twice, once in the shoulder and then in the hip – just "a flesh wound". My father was oblivious to Flash being shot as he drove him to safety. At this point I asked Dad if he had killed any Japanese.

"I like to think I stopped a few," was his reply.

I can only presume that Flash wasn't sent to Alexandra Military Hospital to treat his wounds - otherwise he wouldn't have made it.

Reports from various sources describe events in the battle for Singapore. Dad recalled that frequent reconnaissance was carried out by officers and NCOs to become familiar with the terrain where they would operate, noting the best lines of approach in the forward area. The only brush with the enemy at this time occurred during the nights of February 7th and 8th when the Japanese attacked the island of Ubin which lay in the Straits to the right of the Brigade sector. Ubin was occupied as an outpost by the alternate platoons of C and D companies and the attack happened just as a platoon reached the landing beach, as it usually did, to relieve the occupying platoon.

Around 1,000 enemy soldiers arrived forcing the Platoon back and cutting off four of our men. On the following night a patrol, under Lieutenant PC Barr, went back to the island but found it deserted, with no trace of the four men who had failed to return. That night marked the end of the first phase of the defence of Singapore Island.

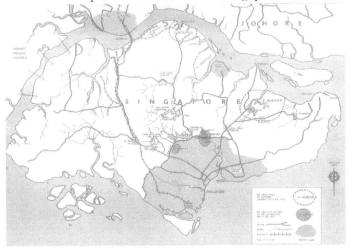

The Norfolks positions in the Battle of Singapore

The second phase of attack – Tomforce

The second phase began when the Japanese made their way along the Straits of Johore, which they had narrowed to about half a mile wide.

That night, they penetrated the forward defences, manned by the Australians, and by the morning of the 9th had advanced around two miles. They then fanned out into a three-pronged attack. The northern prong was aimed at Pierce Reservoir and Seletar Aerodrome, the centre prong at the MacRitchie Reservoir, and the southern one at the village of Bukit Timah.

The following morning, the battalion received orders to form part of a composite force under the command of Lieutenant-Colonel LC Thomas, Royal Northumberland Fusiliers. It was called Tomforce, and its objective was to back up 12 Indian Brigade and to stem the tide of the Japanese advance towards Bukit Timah.

At 12:30 hours the force travelled by bus to the Bukit Timah Road, advancing on the northern side towards the village. On the south side of the road, a similar advance was made by the 5th Sherwood Foresters. That night the Japanese captured the village.

The following morning, the 11th Battalion continued the advance through thickly wooded country on a two-company front. 'A' Company followed by 'D' Company on the left; 'B' Company followed by 'C' Company on the right. There was considerable Japanese activity in the air and as B Company reached its first objective, it was subjected to a low-level bombing attack. Its position was marked by smoke signals dropped by the attacking aircraft, followed by heavy machine gun and mortar fire from concealed Japanese positions. B and C companies both suffered heavy casualties but continued the advance, the carrier platoon giving some support with 2-in-1 mortars. Once again, it ran into heavy opposition with blistering fire from the Japanese on high ground to the North. It was obvious from this attack that the Japanese were infiltrating straight to the North of the Tomforce position, and that their objective was to take the reservoir near Thompson Village.

After consultation with the force commander, it was decided to withdraw the Battalion to the area of Singapore racecourse in an effort to beat back this advance. As good a position as possible was selected and occupied on the right to form a perimeter defence covering the MacRitchie Reservoir. A blunder on the night of the 11th made the situation worse - the 4th Suffolks were ordered to advance towards the Swiss Rifle Club Hill near the junction of the Bukit Timah Road. An objective impossible to reach because of the Japanese strength on the high ground to the North. All it did was to uncover the right flank of the Battalion, a situation which the Japanese took full advantage of. By first light on the 12th the Battalion was almost completely surrounded, with only one small gap left eastward.

At 09:00 hours, the Japanese put in a heavy attack on forward company 'A' which was astride the Bukit Timah Road. The Japanese used tanks in this attack (the Battalion had none), which caused several casualties and forced the company to withdraw. The CO at once planned a counter-attack to restore the position, but before it could be mounted orders were received to withdraw the whole Battalion to Adam Road, running south from the MacRitchie Reservoir. The withdrawal was carried out successfully through the open gap, eastwards of the Battalion positions, with the exception of the carriers which had to run the gauntlet of the Bukit Timah Road. Here they came up against Japanese tanks but successfully fought their way past without loss - a wonderful achievement for the crews who, at one time, had seemed to be facing almost certain annihilation.

Back at Adam Road, Tomforce was dissolved and the Battalion once again came under command of 54th

Infantry Brigade. The strongest defence measures possible were put in place to defend their positions, barbed wire an added deterrent against attacks. It was a reasonably quiet night on 12th-13th February, so it gave some opportunity for the tired troops to catch up on some well-earned sleep. However, this proved to be only the prelude to a heavy attack.

On February 13th, Japanese shelling and mortar fire caused further casualties for the Battalion. The attack itself was largely broken up by fire from supporting artillery, although in the afternoon a further heavy shelling added to the casualties. During the evening, the Battalion was relieved on the western side of Adam Road by the 5th Sherwood Foresters who withdrew into brigade reserve on the east side of the road. Shelling continued throughout the night of 13th-14th February, allowing little sleep and proving that the Japanese were well informed of the Battalion position. The firing became heavier during the morning of the 14th, plus repeated bombing attacks, and again there were many casualties. The Japanese put in several determined attacks, one breaking through to the north of the battalion positions and a second, made in the early hours of the 15th, forcing back the Sherwood Foresters.

By 11:00 hours, B and C companies were ordered to counter-attack and so restored the position, although at a very heavy cost in casualties. In the meantime, the situation of the rest of the island had become critical. The speed of the Japanese advance had been so rapid that 11th (Indian) Division had been overrun and the Commander-in-Chief had been forced to abandon the defence of the Northern beaches. Singapore itself was in a sorry state, its streets choked with the rubble from repeated bombing attacks and the harbour area in a state of chaos as attempts were made to evacuate civilian and non-combatant personnel. As rumour succeeded rumour, it became obvious to all that the end could not be far off. The Battlebox (nickname), formally known as Headquarters Malaya Command Operations Bunker - a bombproof command centre during the Malayan Campaign and the Battle of Singapore - was where all the decisions were made, rightly or wrongly. This is where the statement from Percival was released, stating that every man and woman should do their duty.

"The enemy within our gates must be ruthlessly weeded out."

The help that he needed did not arrive, making his statement worthless.

It has been said by many of those involve at the time that some of the top commanders lacked the 'bottle' to fight the Japanese, but the junior officers wanted to continue the struggle. Lieutenant-General Percival had 90,000 men at his disposal - 17,000 Australians, 33,000 British and 40,000 Indian. The Japanese had approximately 30,000 to 35,000 men with air support, of which we had none. The Japanese constantly bombed Kepple Harbour where, unfortunately, we lost a lot of our equipment.

By this time, the Japanese had control of all the reservoirs on the island. Water was scarce, with only three days of rations left, leaving Percival with little choice. It was clear that all the disagreements between the high command

and junior officers in the Battlebox stayed within the walls of the Battlebox.

The Alexandra Hospital Massacre - 14th-15th February 1942

This was a critical element of the battle for Singapore, with many records of the harrowing events that took place in the hospital.

During the early morning, the water supply was cut off. Shelling and air activity became intense with some of the shells bursting in or near the hospital. These appeared to be mainly Japanese mortar bombs with an occasional shot from artillery. The Japanese were drawing nearer and approaching the rear of the hospital from the Rajah area, Ayer Road. The number of incoming patients had lessened considerably and there was little or no traffic in the wards at this time. During the morning, routine work continued. Japanese troops, the Imperial Japanese Army, the IJA, were seen for the first time at 13:40 hours attacking and moving towards the Sisters' Quarters.

IJA fighting troops were about to enter the hospital from the rear entrance where a white flag had been hoisted to indicate the surrender of the hospital. The Japanese took no notice and Lieutenant Weston, who was carrying the flag of surrender, was bayoneted to death by the first soldier to enter. These troops now entered the hospital and ran riot on the ground floor. They were said to be very excitable and jumpy so that neither pointing to the Red Cross Brassard, nor shouting the word 'hospital', had any effect. One of the Japanese parties entered the Theatre

Block where operations were being prepared in the corridor, between the sisters' bunk and the main theatre, because it was the best lit and most sheltered part of the block. In the operating theatre lay a patient who had been anaesthetized, but the soldier still bayoneting him.

As many statements show, the IJA troops set about bayoneting everybody, including staff and patients who lay in their sick beds. Captain Smiley, Royal Army Medical Corps, kept pointing to the Red Cross Brassard to no avail. He was lunged at with a bayonet but struck the blade aside and it hit the cigarette case in his left breast pocket. He was lunged at once more and wounded in the left groin area, the previous thrust having cut his thumb and wounded his left forearm. He fell to the floor pretending to have been killed. Another group of soldiers went onto a ward demanding that nursing orderlies and patients who could walk should go outside. At the same time, other patients were being bayoneted.

Around 200 patients and personnel were taken outside, their hands tied behind their backs in a slip knot. Some of these patients were tied to four or five other men and could hardly walk. Some seriously ill patients, 'limbless', showed signs of distress, collapsed and had to be revived. They were marched to the old quarters where they were herded into rooms which measured 9x9 feet or 10x12 feet. The Japanese rammed as many men as they could into these rooms so that sitting down was impossible and patients could not avoid urinated against each other. During the night many of these poor souls died. Others were suffering from thirst and the suffocating atmosphere. The soldiers promised water, but it never came.

41

When dawn broke only the Japanese could be seen, many of them with cases of tinned fruit which they kept entirely for themselves. By evening, shelling was at its height and shells were bursting all around. One shell hit the roof of the old quarters injuring some of the prisoners and blowing open the door and windows. When this happened, eight men tried to escape. Some were successful, but others were hit by machine-gun fire. Prior to this, the soldiers had been leading small groups out of sight and the ensuing yells and screams, coupled on one occasion with a Japanese soldier returning wiping blood from his bayonet, left little doubt as to the men's fate. Except for the few who had escaped, none of the party was seen alive again.

There are many more distressing witness accounts of such brutality, including a heavily pregnant orderly being dragged out, bayoneted in the stomach, bringing the foetus out on the end of a bayonet, while they all laughed. Sick. A group of soldiers went into the reception room, shouting and threatening staff and patients who were congregating there - a sergeant was bayoneted along with all the others. Another party of Japanese went into Wards 16 and 17 causing injuries to the patients. They entered the kitchens of these two wards, killing a Private. Once more, they were shown the Red Cross Brassard but replied by firing and throwing a grenade into the sisters' bunk. My father heard from others that the Japanese tied up doctors and nurses in sixes and tossed a grenade into them in front of prisoners. They went about their business murdering everybody.

Surrender

The end came with dramatic suddenness. At around noon on February 15th, a car was seen proceeding along the Bukit Timah Road flying a white flag above a Union Jack. Even though it was thought at first to be a Japanese Fifth Column trick, it had a depressing effect on morale. An hour or so later news was received from Brigade HQ that firing would cease at 16:00 hours, although this was later altered to 20:00 hours. It made little difference to the feeling of bitter disappointment amongst the ranks. The end had indeed come, and the future held only dim and doubtful visions of the unknown horrors of a prison camp. Lieutenant-General Arthur Earnest Percival surrendered Singapore to the Japanese forces under the command of Lieutenant-General Tomoyuki Yamashita. The fall of Singapore was believed to be down to incompetence. We can question whether Percival was a convenient scapegoat.

All that can be said is this: it was Britain's worst wartime disaster.

A leader of men can't lead unless he knows where he is going.

4: The Aftermath

At around 08:00 hours on February 16th, Japanese looters arrived. At 10:00 hours, a Japanese medical officer of the rank of DDMS (Deputy Director of Medical Services) entered the hospital and, incredulously, saluted our dead. He complemented the remaining staff on the way the patients had been looked after and provided a guard against the looters.

The next day, the Japanese Officer in Charge called and expressed regret about what had happened and assured staff that they had nothing further to fear. He also told the OC of the hospital that he was to be regarded as a direct representative of the Emperor, and that no higher honour could be paid to the hospital. It is believed that approximately 280 staff and patients were murdered in the Alexandra Hospital.

When Percival surrendered Singapore, my father told me of the anger and disappointment among the men who wanted to continue the fight. They felt let down but could now see what they were up against. It was noted that one of the reasons Percival surrendered was to protect the civilian population of Singapore. Considering the main population of Singapore was Chinese, and given the atrocities of Unit 731 in Manchuria (see the later section which describes the work of Unit 731), there was little hope left for them. Before the surrender of Singapore, the crucial question was whether anyone in British GHQ had ever received intelligence reports on the IJA's cruelty and

44

barbarism throughout China and Malaya. I personally find this very hard to believe.

Consequently, following surrender, approximately 5000 Chinese were massacred, many beheaded and their heads placed on poles or anything else the Japanese could lay their hands on. If this was intended to demoralise our troops, it certainly worked. Many young men with no experience in warfare realised what they were facing with their captors.

After the surrender, the Battalion and other units of the division congregated in the area of Mount Pleasant, remaining there until February 18th when orders were received from the IJA to march to Changi, a distance of over 20 miles. During the march, one of the halts was at the village of Teck Hock on the Tampines Road, where Battalion HQ had been prior to moving into action on February 10th. Before leaving Teck Hock, all kit had been stacked near Battalion HQ and left under the watchful eye of the first line reinforcements. However, this party was subsequently ordered to join the Battalion and the kit was left without a guard.

Taking advantage of this halt, they visited the kit dump, but found that everything had been rifled through by the locals - men's kit bags had been ripped open and anything useful had been taken. Officers' trunks had completely disappeared. The area was littered with papers and books, most apparently considered of no use. These were burned and the whole scene was carnage. There was, however, one bright spot - an elderly Chinese man came up to the party carrying two pairs of khaki shorts and declared, in very pidgin English, that they had been left by a member of the Battalion for him to wash prior to the Battalion moving from the area. He had them washed and wished to return them. Moreover, he flatly refused to accept any money for his labour, stating that he was only too pleased to be able to help and to hand the shorts over to us. To our guys, such an astonishing case of honesty amidst the surrounding evidence of organised looting was refreshing. I would like to think that this man had survived right up until the Japanese surrendered Singapore back to the British, unlike a further 45,000+ who were murdered throughout Singapore during the Japanese occupation.

5. Changi

Arriving in Changi, the Battalion was quartered in Roberts Barracks. It was quite over-crowded, but the men made the best of it. Rations arrived on trucks of all descriptions and it was at this point that the men were told to hang on to as many of their possessions as possible. While they had something to barter with at the beginning - mainly for food from the locals - it did not take long before most men had bartered all that they had. With no idea at that time how long they would be prisoners of the Japanese, who could blame them?

Once in the barracks, stories of mass cruelty by the Japanese were rife and spread like wildfire. At this point Dad learned of the several thousands of Indian Sikh troops who were defecting and collaborating with the Japanese. He said everyone thought that now the Japanese had taken the 'jewel' in the British Empire, defecting would be beneficial to them in pushing the British out of India. So, these defecting collaborators became guards alongside the Japanese and Koreans in Changi prison and the surrounding areas.

The very first encounter of brutality Dad experienced was not long after the fall of Singapore at Roberts Barracks. He was approached by Japanese and Sikh guards, for no apparent reason, but the look of disgust on my father's face towards the Sikh collaborator was enough for the Japanese guard, who was approximately five feet nothing tall, to slap my father around the face. At this time of capture, Dad was still relatively fit, so he barely flinched on the impact of the

47

slap, which infuriated the Japanese guard so much that he attacked him with his rifle butt. After several blows to the body my father, still on his feet, decided the best course of action would be to drop to the ground where he thought it would be the end. Well, this sadistic bully had other ideas and he started repeatedly kicking him. Dad said that he curled up in the foetal position, with his arms and hands protecting his head and his knees protecting his stomach, letting out a false sickening scream so that the Japanese guard thought he had got the better of him. This certainly worked and as the Japanese guard put in the last kick, he walked away with the Sikh, laughing. Up until the day he told me about this incident, he did not know why he was beaten, only that it was to become a common occurrence throughout his captivity. The Japanese or Koreans did not need an excuse to dish out a beating to any of the prisoners. If any of the guards were unlucky enough to get a slap or a punch from their superiors, then woe betide any prisoner that was close enough to witness this.

Having to bow to the guards was bad enough, but my father found it deeply degrading to have to bow to these collaborators who he had served alongside in India for six and a half years during the 1930s. He felt he could never forgive them for this act of treason. I know now what he meant when he was serving in India and his reference to 'beautiful women but never trust the men'. Obviously, this was his personal view based on these experiences. This is not to take anything away from the loyal Indian army, who, during World War II, had produced the largest volunteer force in history with over 2.5 million men. Many of them would die serving alongside the allied forces, and civilians, on the Death Railway. Their valour was recognised with 4,000 decorations, 38 members of the Indian army receiving the Victoria Cross or the George Cross.

In the barracks, the men were very much left to their own devices under battalion arrangements. The sanitation, cleanliness and discipline of the barracks proceeded along something approaching normal lines. It was at this stage the men were introduced to rice in its most unpalatable form - boiled rice for breakfast, boiled rice for the midday meal and boiled rice in the evening. Each meal was very small. During my travels in the early 70s with Dad from London to Norfolk, I got to meet quite a few Royal Norfolks who were prisoners and very good friends with my father. Jock Symons, who was with him in Roberts Barracks, told me they had a supply of sugar, and Dad was responsible for distributing this amongst the men. Jock stood alongside him while my father gave each man a level spoonful of sugar which had to be exactly equal for every man, almost down to the number of grains! More on Jock later.

The men at this point became extremely resentful to senior officers, questioning why they were in this terrible situation. Junior officers found it hard to bear, blaming the incompetence of senior officers. Percival said, and I quote, "Defences in Singapore are bad for morale of both troops and civilians." I'll let you make up your own minds regarding this statement.

Dad told me that the resilience and discipline of the men was second to none. Hunger was the main issue, as there was a tendency not to eat the disgusting and tasteless rice. Surprisingly, after about a month, the men were in good spirits as they moved from the barracks into the open air adjoining a cricket pitch. Small areas were dry and open but mostly there was a mass of lalang grass, trees, and swamps. The men began to lay foundations on this ground, getting together whatever they could lay their hands on - timber, coconut tree leaves, lalang grass, old tins, just about anything they could get hold of to make life easier for them. Unfortunately, rain, such as experienced in Singapore, took a lot of keeping out, so when it did pour down the makeshift buildings took a battering, as did those who lived in them.

The men made the best of what they had. Garden areas were set up consisting of vegetables such as Chinese radish, sweet potatoes, marrows, and other eastern varieties, mostly unknown - anything to supplement the foul rice. The cricket ground adjoining the open areas was left untouched and to my father's glee was put to normal use, having been a keen amateur cricketer and all-round sportsman. Concert parties, libraries and even a POW university sprang up. Several of the barrack blocks were turned into a hospital to tend to the sick and wounded, however, the medical staff were grossly handicapped by lack of hospital equipment, medicines, and any drugs. When the men wanted to visit the hospital, they had to parade and then be marched to it. This is when the Japanese and defected Indian guards had to be saluted, which the men found degrading.

The supply of water to the camps was well below satisfactory; consumption had to be reduced to a minimum. It wasn't long before the Japanese decided to put the men to work. Working parties were sent down to the docks daily to assist in unloading and loading storerooms, but it worked to their advantage. There was a large supply of tinned food, fruit, tobacco, and cigarettes, which was not affected by fire or shelling. It was amazing how much of this found its way back to camp concealed in any way the prisoners could. Men were also sent out to areas of Singapore to clear the effects of bombing, shelling, and any bodies that were scattered about the place. Dad only spent a few months in Roberts Barracks before being sent up country.

6: Next stop, the Death Railway

Throughout the book, I have not always named the camps where my father and friends experienced complete horror at the atrocities they witnessed, nor do I always give specific times and dates. Why? Well, because the stories told to me by Dad and his mates were often random and I never once asked where and when these atrocities took place. At the time of asking and listening, the geography of Thailand meant nothing to me. It was the stories that held me wide eyed with wonder, the experiences they went through, the atrocities that the Japanese inflicted on them that shocked me to the core. I could not learn enough. I absorbed everything they told to me of these horrific experiences. There were times when names of camps were mentioned, such as Bang Pong, Hintok, Chungkai, Thakhanun, Hell Fire Pass, The Bridge Over The Kwai and Kanburi (as the men called it, short for Kanchanaburi), Allied War Cemetery, and these are the ones I recall most clearly.

Their stories always ended in tears.

My father was in the sixth group of men of about 600 to leave Singapore on June 22nd 1942 to be transported to Thailand, under the command of Lieutenant-Colonel Williamson of the First India HHA (High Hard Armour). Their journey in cattle trucks took about four days.

This was an horrendous journey, the men squeezed into these trucks, barely having the room to sit let alone lay down at night. By day, the metal trucks were like furnaces in the hot sun. Some of the men had already contracted dysentery in the few months spent back in Changi, due to poor diet and contaminated water. Dysentery is an infection of the intestines, a presence of parasitic worms, which manifests itself as constant diarrhoea containing blood or mucus. Other symptoms include abdominal pain, nausea, vomiting, fever, and a feeling of incomplete defecation. There are two types of dysentery, amoebic and bacillary, the latter being the deadliest of the two.

By night, the trucks became extremely cold. It was to be four days with very little rice and water, the men getting progressively weaker, hardly having any sleep, and surrounded by the putrid smell of faeces and urine. Picture yourself in this position and how you would have coped. The weakest of men were passing out, relying on their comrades for help as they arrived at Ban Pong, Thailand on the June 26th 1942, the starting point of the 'Death Railway' as we have all come to know it. I shall always refer to it as such because that is exactly what it was then, and how it should always be known, in honour of those that built it and those that died.

Ban Pong was a filthy transit camp. Dad noticed that the working parties that had left Singapore before him were in a very poor state. Many working parties disembarked at Ban Pong, weakened by the four-day train journey, facing long route marches to camps further along the Death Railway. There were a few men on these marches that never made it to their destination, and quite a few that took beatings along the way. It doesn't come as any surprise that men in such poor health, being marched up to 200 miles, fell by the wayside. Ban Pong was also the base camp for all the Death Railway parties arriving from Singapore, at the time the only hospital in Thailand for prisoners.

The camp was split into two - on one side of the road was the permanent camp and the other was for transit. In the rainy season, the camp was ankle deep in mud and excreta - it was a quagmire. The latrines were a deep trench, with bamboo stretched across. This left the men with no privacy and it did not take long for the maggots to infest the whole area. The whole camp was then plagued by giant bluebottles and dysentery became rife. Furthermore, the hospital was in the lowest part of the camp and was often flooded. In Attap huts[1], patients were laying on bamboo structures 6 feet long and 18 inches wide, and only a few inches from the flooding water. To those that were struck down with dysentery, more illness was to strike them. Mosquitos took over the area at night and malaria[2] soon took hold of the men.

As if dysentery and malaria were not enough, the worst was yet to come.

---

[1] Attap huts are named after the Attap Palm which provides leaves for the roofs on a bamboo structure with open sides.

[2] Malaria is a mosquito-borne infectious disease affecting humans. Without treatment, symptoms include, fever, fatigue, vomiting, headaches, yellowing of the skin, seizures, coma, or death.

7: Working on the Death Railway

It is useful to note the basic details about the Railway to set the context for the work of prisoners.

The Burma Railway – often referred to as the 'Death Railway' - is a 415-kilometre (258 miles) railway between Ban Pong, Thailand and Thanbyuzayat, Burma. It was designed by the Japanese and built by the POWs and civilian workers to support its forces in the Burma campaign. Construction of the 'Death Railway' started in October 1942 and was finished in the remarkably short period of just 12 months.

Romusha is a Japanese language word for labourer but has come to denote specifically forced labourers during the Japanese occupation of the Far East.

Along the Death Railway were roughly 76 prisoner of war camps (but note that names of some of these camps have since altered). Many horrific stories have been told of the sadistic and cruel atrocities carried out in these camps along the Death Railway.

The full list of camps is in the Appendix, but the following are some of the main ones:

Nong Pla Duk - start of construction in June 1942	Ban Pong - transit camp and first P.O.W hospital
Tha Rua Noi - transit camp for prisoners marching North	Kanchanaburi - Kanburi to the men. war cemetery, hospital camp
Khwae Yai Bridge Bridge of the River Kwai	Chungkai - war cemetery, main hospital camp, POW camp

Wang Po - the Wampo viaduct	Thasao - HQ and hospital
Tonchan - commenced work here on arrival from Singapore May 1943	Kannyu - POWs from this camp worked on the infamous Hell Fire Pass
Kuiyae - Dutch POWs killed in allied bombing 1944	Yongthi - Australian and Dutch camp
Kroeng Krai - six Australians killed in a rock fall	Sonkrai - Australian camp of 400 men, suffered many deaths
Chaunggahiaya - British camp, 214 died here, buried in a single mass grave	Apalon Bridge - site of one of the seven steel railway bridges
Apalaine - base hospital	Tanngzun - dead Asians found in huts, start of Cholera epidemic
Thanbaya - desperately sick brought here from Thailand, 700 died in less than 6 months	Beketaung - 184 Americans arrived here October 1942
Retphaw - became base hospital after repeated bombings at Thambyuzayat	Thanbuyuzayat - War cemetery, base hospital camp

Between 180,000 and 250,000 South East Asian civilian labourers (Romusha), and about 61,000 allied POWs, were subjected to forced labour during the railway's construction. Roughly 100,000 civilian labourers and more than 12,000 allied prisoners of war died - one died for every sleeper laid.

To build the 'Death Railway' between October 1942 and October 1943, the Japanese needed a larger workforce than just the allied prisoners. The hundreds of thousands of Asian unskilled native labourers (no one knows the exact number), 'coolies', were press-ganged by the Japanese and their surrogates to work on the railway. These included Tamils, Chinese and Malayans from colonial Malaya, Burmese from present day Myanmar, and others from what is now Indonesia. With the promise of better living conditions, wages and food, the Death Railway would be a glorious project that would help liberate India from the grip of the British Colonists. Some went voluntarily, others were forced by the Japanese along with their allied troops.

These 'coolies' became slave labour. Approximately 100,000 died from malnutrition and disease, their camps along the Death Railway were appalling and in a terrible state, and there was no medical assistance. Unlike the POWs who retained the military hierarchical system of officers and enlisted men, the Asian workers were disorganised. The POWs were kept separate from the Asian labourers. Bodies of hundreds of ill and emaciated Asian labourers were thrown into mass graves, some of them not yet dead. Witnesses said they were still groaning when they threw them into the hole.

February 24th 1944, the Japanese built a monument at Ban Makham to comfort the soul and spirit of the labourers and captives who died building the railway. Words are written in eight foreign languages on all four corners of the monument praising the 'goodness' and 'kindness' of the labourers. It is truly beyond belief to praise those whom you have starved, beaten and murdered.

The Japanese treated all these 'coolies' as slave labourers, having no regard for them at all. Just like the Chinese of Manchuria, our own POWs meant little to the Japanese – finally the situation is becoming recognized as the forgotten Holocaust. Today along with the Chinese they are still fighting for compensation.

Comfort Women

One story was only briefly mentioned until fairly recently - that of the 'Comfort' women. Between 1932 and 1945 Japan forced women from Korea, China, and the Philippines into sexual slavery. Comfort women were used as military sexual slaves in occupied territories. The word 'comfort' women is a translation of the Japanese word 'ianfu' (comfort) and is a euphemism for prostitute. Estimates vary as to how many women were involved, with numbers ranging from as low as 20,000 (this number comes from a Japanese historian, Ikuhiko Hata), but evidence shows there were many more. The real figure is could easily be as high as 360,000 - 410,000. The exact numbers are still being researched and debated.

'Comfort Stations' (brothels) were located in Japan, China, the Philippines, Indonesia, Malaya, Thailand, Burma, New Guinea, Hong Kong, Macau and French Indo-China. A smaller number of women of European origin, mostly from the Netherlands and Australia were also involved, with an estimated 200-400 Dutch women alone. According to testimonies, young women were abducted from their homes in countries under Imperial Japanese rule. In many cases women were lured with a promise of work in factories or restaurants, or opportunities for higher education (just as the men were in recruiting for the Death Railway).

A better life for all.

Once the women had been recruited, they were incarcerated in Comfort Stations, at home and abroad. Approximately three quarters of comfort women died, and most survivors were left infertile due to sexual trauma or sexually transmitted diseases. Moreover, beatings and physical torture were said to be common. Girls of 13 and 14 years of age were "broken in" by being repeatedly raped. Some women were raped 30-40 times a day every day of the year. The Japanese testified that the comfort women were seen as "female ammunition" and "public toilets", as, literally, things to be used and abused. Some comfort women were forced to donate blood for the treatment of wounded soldiers. The Dutch women were taken by force from prison camps in Java by officers of the Imperial Japanese Army. They were systematically beaten and raped day and night, while those who refused to comply were murdered. During the last stand of Japanese forces in 1944-1945 comfort women were often forced to commit suicide or were killed.

In Burma, there were cases of Korean comfort women committing suicide by swallowing cyanide pills or by hand grenades tossed into their dugouts. British soldiers fighting in Burma often reported that the Korean comfort women whom they captured were astonished to learn that the British were not going to eat them as they had been told by the Japanese. Ironically, given this claim, there were cases of starving Japanese troops cut off on remote Pacific

Islands or trapped in the jungles of Burma turning towards cannibalism. In addition, there were at least several cases where comfort women in Burma and on Pacific Islands were murdered to provide protein for the Imperial Japanese Army. The Japanese now had slaves all over South East Asia.

Throughout Thailand, Comfort Stations were being set up. Thai traders were also involved by bringing young Thai prostitutes up-river on barges full of rice sacks, fruit, and vegetables, stopping at various camps along the River Kwai. These girls, although prostitutes, were once used to preoccupy a Japanese guard who, along with five or six POWs, was at the docking area waiting to unload the barges. This gave the trader time to trade secretly with the POWs and inform them of the latest news. Some of these Thai traders belonged to V organisation, operating out of Bangkok, who supplied "with great risk" much needed medicines, money, and food. These items were sewn into the rice sacks that the prisoners unloaded off the barges and hid whilst the Japanese guard was pleasuring himself in the bushes. Without the help of this organization, life would have been so much harder and there would definitely have been more deaths in the hospital camps along the Death Railway. I do not know if these girls were recognised for their duty after the war, all I know is if they weren't, they should have been.

8: Suffering and horror as a FEPOW

As already said, the start of my father's journey as a Japanese prisoner of war began with his capture in Singapore on February 15th 1942. In May 1942, some 3,000 Australian men, known as A Force, left Changi to work on airfields in Southern Burma. In late June 1942, a force of 600 British POWs (Work Group 2) had been moved to Ban Pong to begin preliminary work on the Thailand side. Dad, who arrived here in cattle truck on 26th June from Changi, would have been a part of this workforce. Ban Pong was a filthy transit camp, 3.3 kilometres up the railway - essentially, the beginning of it.

In September 1942, they were moved to Thanbyuzayat, the northern starting point of the Death Railway. In November 1942, Dad was moved up country, 81.3 kilometres, to Wan Takhian until April 1943. From this time, he was moved even further up the railway by some 225 kilometres to Thakanun, recorded as "pretty frightful here". In October 1943, he was sent down the line to Chunkai, a work camp and one of the main hospital camps. Now known as Chunkai POW Cemetery, it is located on the same spot as the Chunkai camp, on the banks of the Kwai Noi River. Nakhon Pathom, a very large POW hospital camp with 10,000 beds, was set up by the Japanese in December 1943 to handle chronic and heavily sick patients. This camp was to be my father's last until liberation on 4th September 1945.

Lieutenant-Colonel Ishii was the Japanese commandant at Nakhon Pathom. Lieutenant-Colonel

Sainter was the POW administrative officer, and Lieutenant-Colonel Albert Coates AIF the Chief Medical Officer. He gathered around him many of the best British, Australian, and Dutch surgical and medical officers throughout Thailand. Lieutenant-Colonel 'Weary' Dunlop arrived from Chunkai to join this team, along with Major Sydney Kranz, recorded as the Senior Visiting Surgeon in the camp at that time. Here Lieutenant-Colonel Coates, a very busy man of course with his enormous responsibilities, was known to be involved in more serious cases, such as amputations.

My initial research led me to believe that my father's surgery took place at Nakhon Pathom, however, further research showed he was operated on to remove a duodenal ulcer at Chungkai on 14th July 1944. He was operated on by Major Pembleton and anaesthetist/assistant, Captain Welsh. Six weeks later he was transported 72 Kms in infested, unsanitary conditions, across savage terrain to Nakhon Pathom, his final camp. It wasn't long before Nakhon Pathom hospital camp became full. Seriously sick and dying POWs were transported from camps all along the Death Railway by train, road, and barges down the River Kwai. To some, this was to become God's waiting room.

At Changi, the POWs had had very little contact with the Japanese, discipline among the men coming from their own officers. In Thailand they were suddenly thrown into direct and violent contact with the Japanese engineers and the Korean guards.

Some experiences of cruelty were common to all workforces sent to Burma and Thailand in 1942-1943.

Daily beatings were an everyday occurrence in all the camps along the Death Railway, some more severe than others. Men would suffer broken limbs due to the severity of the beating. The guards would use rifle butts, clubs (bamboo) and fists upon weakened men, starving and sick men who might have forgotten to bow to them or were not working hard enough - any excuse to dish out punishment.

In the many beatings my father witnessed, the guards were not content with just knocking a man to the ground, they would then proceed to kick him until unconscious, laughing in many cases. It sickened my father to watch these beatings even though he would succumb to a few beatings himself during his captivity.

There was one incident among many that would have an everlasting impression on Dad. During the early days of construction on the railway he, along with five other men from the camp, were sent to work on a clearing to prepare their section. This meant that, with only a chunkel (a form of shovel) and basket, the men would have to break up rocks and anything else that was in the way ready for the railway sleepers to be laid. One of the men was a 6ft 4in prisoner, with bright ginger hair. My father described him as a colossus of a man, having not lost too much weight since his capture in February 1942.

Two Korean guards took it upon themselves to goad this man, having never seen a giant of a man with bright ginger hair. Both laughing, they set about jabbing him with fixed bayonets, enough to pierce the skin. There was nothing my father or the other men could do but watch this poor guy being tormented by these sick, sadistic monsters. Prodding and jabbing him took its toll to the point where he could take no more. Within seconds, he grabbed both guards and threw them down the bank to their deaths.

My father and the other men stood still, surrounded by Japanese guards screaming at them while beating them to the ground. The prisoner took an immense beating to the point of unconsciousness. All six men were dragged away into the jungle by the guards. By the time they got to a clearing the prisoner had regained consciousness and my father thought this was the end for them all. The Japanese however, had other ideas.

The beatings stopped but the screaming at the men continued. One guard was sent away, while the others stripped the prisoner naked and tied him down. Along with the other men, Dad was made to stand in line about 15 feet away from the poor soul. The guard who had been sent away reappeared carrying a small sack filled with sugar. The men watched as the guard poured the sugar all over the man's body. Red ants appeared from nowhere and within 15 seconds had engulfed his whole body. His screams were to stay with my father for the rest of his life.

Red ants, known as fire ants, bite to get a grip and then sting (from their abdomen) and inject a toxic alkaloid venom. To humans, this is a painful sting, hence the name fire ant, and the after-effects of the sting can be deadly to sensitive individuals. Once the red ants had left the body, my father and the other men were marched back to work, while the body of the prisoner was left in the jungle never to be seen again.

By this time, malaria and dysentery had really taken hold of the men, yet the Japanese refused to recognise malaria as an illness, still sending those that were racked with the disease to work on the railway. 12-hour days were soon stretched from 7:30 in the morning after tenko (roll call) till 9 or 10 o'clock in the evening, as the Japanese engineers had set a deadline for the completion of the Death Railway.

Desperately sick prisoners from camps along the railway were pulled from their sick beds in hospitals to make up the numbers. The soldiers had no regard for human life just as long as this railway was completed on time. Even able-bodied men, though emaciated and starving and working 12-16 hours a day, would soon join the seriously sick. Working days consisted of breaking rocks and removing them and bamboo cutting. This was always a constant threat to the men because the bamboo, when cut down, left very sharp edges that would either scratch or pierce their legs causing ulcers. Work also included tree felling, bridge building, embankment building, pile driving in blazing tropical heat. All these jobs were made even more dangerous during the monsoon season (torrential rain) as many men fell to their death while working on the viaducts and bridges.

At the same time, the soldiers informed the POW officers that the men should look after their health. On many occasions, officers and medical staff would ask for medical supplies, which always fell on deaf ears, and consequently resulted in beatings for asking. After one of these long days, when the men returned to their camp, Dad noticed a man walking aimlessly round and round talking to himself. Before anyone could help the poor man, he was surrounded by Korean and Japanese guards laughing at him. There was nothing the men could do to help him.

65

The man had lost his mind and was laughing along with the guards.

One guard, who had had enough, stopped laughing and rifle butted him in the head. He fell to his knees still laughing. When the other guards joined in, repeatedly beating him until he keeled over in an unconscious bloody mess, the guards walked away laughing. The men quickly got him into the sick bay but, unfortunately, there was nothing they could do to help. His injuries were so severe that he died not long afterwards. I would like to think that this was a release for this lost soul.

Stories of brutal beatings and murder were rife as men were moved from camp to camp along the route of the Death Railway. Being moved was also a time to catch up with some of Dad's mates from the same regiment, separated at some point between Changi or other camps. It was also a time to learn that some of his mates had not made it and had been buried at Chungkai or Kanchanaburi war cemeteries. My father told me once that he hoped I would never experience true friendship like he experienced. By this, he meant I wouldn't have to go through what he went through - when your mate would lay down his life for yours! So, when it came to catching one of your own stealing off another, my father was appalled.

One evening, he was told by a member of the medical staff in the camp that a mate of his in the hospital hut was in a very bad way and might not make it through the night. Straight away, my father made his way over to be with him along with another pal from the Norfolks. As they approached the hospital in darkness, they noticed a prisoner fumbling about between the sick beds. It was still in the early stages of captivity when most of the lucky men still had boots but, clearly, this man didn't. My father and his mate caught him stealing a pair of boots off a very sick man. The soldier was from the Manchester Regiment. In the morning he was also a patient in the hospital, ironically lying in the next bed to the guy from whom he stole the boots.

All Dad said was that this guy would think twice before he stole off one of his own again. He dealt with him as if he were the lowest of the low. When two men from the same regiment (Manchester) were caught red-handed stealing food off the sick, lowest of the low took on a whole new meaning and these men were 'dealt with' internally. They were disgraced among the other men in the camp who had nothing more to do with them. Fortunately, there were not many of these incidents, but there would always be a rotten apple among the many.

Once when my father and I were alone in our living room I watched as a wry smile appeared on his face. I was about to ask him what he was thinking about, but he beat me to it. He would go into a world of his own on many occasions, but this time was different. He was smiling when he told me of two Japanese guards that were brothers and had been educated in England before the war; both spoke very good English. They had found out that Dad was a regimental boxing champion, although how that happened, I don't know, and didn't ask him as I was too enthralled listening to the story that he was about to tell me! They wanted my father to teach them boxing. Boxing wasn't a Japanese art and obviously these brothers would have learnt about the sport while studying back in England. As weak as he was, he could do nothing but agree to train them.

After tenko, they would take him into the jungle where he started by teaching them the basics of boxing, that is the stance, bending of the knees, elbows tucked in protecting the body and head. Dad burst out laughing recalling both brothers were as "bandy as coots." Teaching them the basics wasn't going to be easy. Each daily lesson lasted about an hour. After the lessons, the brothers gave Dad a small tin of condensed milk and a tin of fruit, which he distributed among the men when he returned to camp, making him very popular. While training the brothers, they never possessed boxing gloves, so my father would tie rags around their hands. When it came to sparring with the little knowledge they had been taught, he paired them, stood back, and watched the brothers try to rip each other's heads off. Highly amusing for my Dad. In fact, he would often have to jump in and separate them. He thought he had better spar with each one separately, which he didn't want to do in the beginning because of any reprisals if he hurt them.

They were both very eager to learn the art of boxing. The more the lessons went on, the more tins of milk and fruit my father received, so he took his time in training them. These two were the worst pupils in the history of boxing. Even though highly educated, they could not grasp the art at all. Everything my father had tried to teach them went out of the window. My father took over the sparring and as he would jab one of the brothers on the chin, the other brother would laugh so much at him being hit that all hell would break loose and they would start slapping and kicking each other. The ironic thing was, after each lesson, they both bowed to my father and thanked him and then promptly marched him back to camp and resumed their duties.

One day, after the lesson had finished and they returned to camp, my father saw another side to the two brothers, which in a way came as no surprise to him. After all, they were his captors. They punched and kicked a prisoner who had got in their way and made him hold a large rock above his head in the blazing heat until he passed out. The next day after tenko, one brother came over to Dad to say the boxing lessons were over as his brother had gone down with malaria (remember this is a disease the Japanese did not recognise) and was being sent down country. Although he was going to miss the tins of milk and fruit, he was glad to wash his hands of these two and he never saw them again.

9. Just Trying to Survive

As the months of working on the Death Railway between October 1942 until completion in October 1943 rolled on, approximately 100,000 men had died, either through malnutrition, beatings, sheer exhaustion, or disease. Along the 415 kilometres of the railway, many men suffered tropical ulcers, mainly to the legs, including my father. These ulcers would eat deep into the flesh, exposing bone. To save ulcerated legs, Dad told me that they would heat up a spoon to scoop out the infection, then place maggots to the infected area to eat away the rotten flesh. This saved many from losing limbs, but others were not so lucky.

This is when the medical teams came into their own, saving many lives by amputations despite the lack of medical supplies. Each and every one of the medical staff working in these camps, in appalling conditions yet saving so many lives, deserved every accolade their countries could bestow on them. By now, dysentery had really taken hold amongst the men. Latrines were a dug-out trench, with a bamboo structure above consisting of two poles stretched along the trench for the men to sit on. These were disgusting places constructed away from the huts due to the stench, maggots, and blue bottles.

One night a mate of my father's, as weak as he was, made his way to the latrines and sat on the poles to relieve himself when he heard a faint cry for help. Beneath him, laying in the trench, covered in excrement, maggots, and flies, was a prisoner who was obviously extremely weak and had slipped between the poles into the trench. Not knowing how long this poor guy had been lying there, he tried in vain to pull him out, but he kept slipping from his weakened grasp. As quickly as he could, he went to seek help. When he and two other men returned to get him out of the trench, he was in a dreadful state. They managed to get him to the hospital hut where, within a few days, he made a recovery. However, as they would later discover, he died of cholera a year later. Dad told me that you didn't know when it was your time, you just got on with it and hoped for the best.

To supplement their very poor diet of boiled, tasteless rice, lacking any kind of vitamins, they would do anything they could to barter with the local Thais, who took extreme risks to help the prisoners. If caught by the guards they would receive a severe beating or would even be killed. Every sack of rice that was delivered by barge up the River Kwai to the camps would contain weevils (a form of beetle), which laid its eggs in the rice. Once the rice was boiled, the men would pick out the weevils. Adding anything to this pulp was a bonus.

In one of the camps where my father was interned, the Commandant had a pet pig which managed to get loose from its compound and run through the camp. Within no time, this pig was clubbed over the head, buried by the prisoners, with the aim to dig it up later that night and give it to the cooks in the cookhouse. In the meantime, the Commandant was going berserk about his missing pig. He ordered all the guards in the camp to search for it, to the amusement of the prisoners. The leading POW officer of the camp was called to the Commandant's hut regarding the whereabouts of his beloved pig. He explained to him, through an interpreter, that the men had seen the pig run into the jungle. That was the end of that. That night, both the sick and the able tasted pork among their rice. There wasn't a bit of that pig that was wasted.

Snake also became a much-needed protein to be added to the rice. Even though Thailand has 35 listed dangerous snakes, including cobras, kraits, keel backs, vipers, and coral snakes - they were considered a delicacy. Of course, the men had to be very careful catching them. Dad saw a couple of Australian prisoners, who were quite used to handling dangerous snakes back home, pick up a snake by its tail and before it could coil or strike, swing it around with great speed to crack its head against anything hard to kill it. They were soon thrown into the cooking pot (a bit like jellied eels without the jelly). Those that were bitten by one of these snakes died a horrible death. It is not recorded how many died from snake bites. Rats, which were in abundance and a lot easier to catch than snakes, were also to become part of the staple diet for the prisoners. Their main source of food came from the local Thais.

This brings me to another story that sickened me as a young man. A Thai girl of about 18 years of age visited the camp nightly with her wares of dried fish, eggs, and all sorts of fruit, to barter out of sight of the Japanese and Korean guards. She was a very pretty girl with a lovely smile and the dangers of being caught didn't seem to faze her; she was a very brave girl. Bartering at this point became more and more difficult as the men's resources were drying up. At first, the men had some money, watches (which they had hidden), and any part of their uniforms, which the Thais loved getting their hands on. However, they soon had hardly any money left and certainly no gold, silver, or watches, plus the uniforms at this point were in a pretty poor state. So, they turned to their boots. Boots to many men were nonexistent, but the men did the best they could with what they had left to barter with and if this was all they had, then so be it.

This young girl's luck was about to run out. She always had a set time to visit the camp's perimeter at night, which made it easier for the prisoners, so everybody would be on alert to avoid being captured. One evening, as the men were approaching the exact spot to meet up with the girl, they heard her screams in the distant jungle. They knew she had been captured and dreaded the thought of what would become of her. They quickly returned to their huts in case they were caught as well.

Many nights passed without any trading, or any news of the young girl, until about two weeks later when a prisoner going to the latrines heard a voice from the perimeter. The Japanese and Korean guards always stayed clear of the latrines, mostly because of the smell and catching anything nasty. Having finished his business, he went over to where he had heard the voice of an old man. He was standing there with a basket of fruit, eggs, and some dried fish and could speak enough pidgin English to be understood. The prisoner asked him what had happened to the young girl. It turned out that she was his niece and she had been caught by the Korean guards who beat her black and blue and continually raped her. They, along with the Kempeitai (see the later chapter), took the girl back to the village not far from the camp where she lived. The Kempeitai tore the hut apart where she lived with her family, beating every family member close to death. The uncle managed to get away before being noticed. The young girl the Kempeitai took away from her village was never seen again. No-one knew what became of her.

After the atrocity of the young girl, Dad was told that bathing in the river and any trading was forbidden. If life in the camps wasn't hard enough, it was going to become even harder. One prisoner caught stealing a banana was decapitated, and many others were beaten unconscious if suspected of stealing. At this time, the Japanese needed every man available to complete the Death Railway, so you do question why they beat them if not for their own twisted perversion. Hospitals along the railway route were raided by the IJA for any men that could stand (for how long was immaterial). The phrase "speedo" (faster, faster) rang through the men's ears. The weak that were brought out of the hospitals were, inevitably, the first to fall. During the last few weeks of construction, the men were dead on their feet with malnutrition, vitamin deficiency diseases, beri-beri, malaria, tropical ulcers, and dysentery. But, by October 1943 the men, including my father, came through it.

The Death Railway was completed at the cost of over 100,000 men.

10. You cannot break their spirit

My father and many others, from Changi, Ban Pong, Wan Lun, Wan Taknian and Thakhanun had experienced and seen it all - beatings, torture, and death. But even then, their flames had not been completely doused and occasionally some amusing comments from the men would raise a laugh.

One such moment was when one of Dad's friends was being shaved around the genitals because he was covered with many forms of body lice. These would constantly bite, worse than mosquitoes, and so, by becoming hairless, it helped relieve the discomfort. The allocated camp barber had the pleasure (for want of a better word) of shaving the men and while removing his pubic hair with a very blunt cut-throat razor, he accidentally nicked his penis. Holding his manhood, he said to the barber, "What the bleedin' 'ell 'ave you done?" The barber said, "I wouldn't worry mate, you won't be using that for a while", which caused great mirth amongst the men standing behind him in the queue waiting to be shaved.

Another amusing moment occurred in one of the hospital huts where prisoners were suffering from bouts of malaria. Dad heard that a prisoner had just been brought in from a brutal beating by the Japanese guards. They had beaten him with sticks until he fell to the ground where they proceeded to kick him in the nether regions. Lying on a hospital bed, the doctors set about doing all they could to help him, all the while he had both hands on his privates. Even though this guy was badly beaten, it did not stop his

British sense of humour. Referring to his swollen and painful testicles and penis, he asked the doctor for some pills to take away the pain but leave the swelling. Those that could laugh, laughed out loud including my father.

The Japanese broke the prisoners' bodies but never ever their spirit.

By now the men's uniforms had more or less disintegrated, leaving them to come up with some sort of clothing to cover their dignity. Along came the option of the only material available to them, the making of the 'Jap Happy,' which was a rectangular piece of cloth tied around the waist, passed between the legs and tucked under the cord; very similar to what Sumo Wrestlers would wear, a glorified nappy. Without any protection on their feet, trench foot became a problem, and Dad also suffered from trench foot.

Trench foot is a medical condition caused by prolonged exposure of the feet to damp, unsanitary, and cold conditions. Affected feet may become numb by erythema (turning red) or cyanosis (turning blue) due to poor blood supply, and may begin emanating a decaying odour if the early stages of necrosis (tissue death) sets in. As the condition worsens, feet may also begin to swell. Advanced trench foot often involves blisters and open sores, which lead to fungal infections. This is sometimes called tropical ulcers (tropical rot). If left untreated, trench foot usually results in gangrene, which may require amputation. If trench foot is treated properly, complete recovery is normal, though it is marked by severe short-term pain when feelings return.

11. Thakhanun camp.

The last camp my father was in before being sent to Chungkai was Thakhanun, arriving here in April 1943. This was an appalling camp. The men were in very poor health and food was scarce to the point of rationing. Some men were living in tents while others were out in the open. Four deaths a day were recorded here, so I can only imagine that those seven months my father was there, with the ever-present words of "speedo, speedo" ringing out to complete the Death Railway even faster, were horrific.

One evening, when I was alone with my father, he mentioned the outbreak of cholera in the camps. There was a long pause. I could see this was very upsetting for him to discuss with me, so I sat there watching him gather his thoughts before he continued. Not once during all our talks did he ever have eye contact with me. It was as if I wasn't even in the room. I got to the stage where I didn't interrupt him, sitting absorbing everything he told me. This particular evening was more emotional than the others. I have no idea what year or what camp my father was in when he experienced this outbreak of cholera, only that the more he spoke about it his tears would flow. I hated watching this strong man, who I loved very much, break down.

He told me the story of his mate contracting the disease and within hours he was unrecognisable. Not long after sitting with him, he died. It was only when he told me that his friend was then placed in a rice sack and he set him alight that my father became inconsolable. So, I put my arms around him for solace. The reason for cremating those that died from cholera was that it was extremely contagious, with a high mortality rate which caused about 12% of overall prisoner deaths. Spread by food and water contaminated by faeces, it was prevalent in the wet season when the latrines overflowed. The symptoms were horrific. With severe loss of fluid, cholera victims became unrecognisable in only a few hours. Victims were tagged when diagnosed so that they could be identified later. They were also segregated in separate huts or camps where possible. Those who died were immediately cremated.

With deaths occurring most days during the "speedo" period of mid-1943, each camp had its own rough cemetery. Medical personnel kept details of the grave sites of the dead so that their bodies could be recovered, and identified, later. I can only assume through my research that the story Dad told me happened at Thakhanun, known as a cholera camp.

12. Chunkai and Nakhon Pathom camps

In October 1943, my father was sent down country to Chunkai where the conditions were better than Thakhanun. It was here that he was to learn of the death of one of his mates, Lesley Leonard Rice, who is buried in Chunkai War Cemetery. This catching-up with the news was a daily occurrence between the men, as they were moved from camp to camp and asking the whereabouts of their mates from the same regiments. Some were lucky and reunited with their pals. Others were told that their mates had either been murdered or died, working on the Death Railway, through starvation or disease. Once the railway was completed many prisoners were sent back to Changi, Singapore, where life was a lot easier for them than the last year and a half in Thailand. Many others were not so lucky.

They were to be sent to Japan to work, mainly in coal mines, transported in what became known as the 'hell ships.' Even though the railway was complete, it still had to be maintained by the prisoners left in Thailand. There was still a lot of work to be done, so the Japanese did not ease up on the cruelty. The men's body weight was dropping rapidly. There was to be no respite for the men as the railway had to be maintained, as well as cutting and building roads, some of it in terrible virgin jungle.

While in Chungkai, my father, part of Work Group 2, was listed in Japan Party 2, leaving Singapore from River Valley Road on July 4th 1944. He was to be on one of these hell ships, Hakushika Maru, heading for Japan to work in the coal mines, along with six other ships during July. Conditions on board these ships were appalling, causing much suffering and even death. Many were sunk by allied shipping or air attacks, unaware that they were carrying prisoners of war.

Unfortunately, but perhaps fortunately, Dad fell seriously ill in Chungkai which stopped him from making this terrible journey and, quite probably, saved his life. In August 1944, he was transported to the very large hospital camp of Nakhon Pathom. His admission to the hospital of this camp is recorded as 20th August 1944, suffering from a burst duodenal ulcer, tropical ulcers, malaria, trench foot and PUO. This medical abbreviation refers to a pyrexia (fever) of unknown origin, used when a patient has a fever, but the cause has not yet been diagnosed. He was operated on immediately by Major Pembleton and Captain Welsh, who removed the burst ulcer as well as a large section of his stomach, all with handmade surgical tools and whatever resources they could lay their hands on.

I remember saying to my father, "Dad, you have got to be the only prisoner that returned home with a map of the Death Railway on your chest and abdomen". That's exactly what his scar looked like. After the operation, he was placed under observation by the medical orderlies. He was in a bad way for a long time, and it was touch and go whether he pulled through. His two friends were to play a major role in his recovery. Each night, they would take it in turns to sit with him, while he was still unconscious, and read aloud *Gone with the Wind* by Margaret Mitchell. This went on for quite a while until he regained consciousness. All this must have had a psychological effect on him. Early in 1946, Dad took my mother to watch the film of *Gone with the Wind* at The Elephant and Castle in South East London. He never went to the cinema again. I have no idea how long it took Dad to recover to some sort of normality, but Nakhon Pathom was to be his last camp until liberation on 4th September 1945.

13: Liberation

At Nakhon Pathom camp, just before the Japanese surrender, the men knew that their time in captivity was drawing to an end. But what end? Freedom or death? The mood in the camp among the guards made everyone jumpy. Then, one morning, the prisoners awoke to discover that their captors had left during the night. There was not a Japanese or Korean soldier in sight. In the camp men were cheering and crying - at last they were free men again. Yet they still had to stay, waiting in the camp until help and transport arrived. The cooks were given orders to cook-up whatever they could lay their hands on. As the soldiers had left in a hurry, they left their own food supplies, so the cooks had a field day and the men were very grateful.

It could have been very different if the Japanese had carried out their orders. Prisoners had already been made to dig trenches around the perimeters of each camp, as mass graves, and the orders had been given to exterminate every prisoner along the Death Railway having just dug their own graves. From the time of Japanese surrender my father, along with all the other prisoners at Nakhon Pathom, had a two week wait before being liberated. During that time some of the very sick died.

They died free men.

During the months leading up to liberation, the prisoners could hear bombing in the distance, gradually getting closer to Nakhon Pathom camp. Bangkok was about 56.4 km away, roughly 31 miles, and was being bombed by the Allies on numerous occasions. From May 1945, Blenheim Bombers and Mustangs flew from Rangoon to bomb Bangkok. The Japanese command centre for the Far East was based in Bangkok until the end of the war in August that year. In Europe, the Germans surrendered on May 8th so the Allies turned their full attention to the Far East. The Allied forces called for the unconditional surrender of the Imperial Japanese Armed Forces in the Potsdam Declaration on July 26th 1945, the alternative being 'prompt and utter destruction'. Japan ignored the ultimatum and the war with them continued. On August 6th the first atomic bomb was dropped on Hiroshima and three days later a second bomb was dropped on Nagasaki. The bombs immediately devastated their targets.

Japan's Emperor Hirohito announced his country's unconditional surrender in a radio address on August 15th citing the devastating power of a new and most cruel bomb.

Operation Tiderace

Operation Tiderace was the code name of the British plan to retake Singapore, in coordination with Operation Zipper which involved the liberation of Malaya.

Following the Japanese surrender in 1945, the liberation force was led by Lord Louis Mountbatten, Supreme Allied Commander of South East Asia Command. On August 20th General Seishiro Itagaki, the Commander of Singapore, signalled to Lord Mountbatten that he would abide by his Emperor's decision, and he was

83

ready to receive instructions for the Japanese surrender of Singapore onboard HMS Sussex on September 4th 1945. Allied troops set sail for Singapore from Trincomalee and Rangoon on August 31st. On September 12th, Lord Mountbatten signed the Acceptance of Surrender.

Itagaki met his generals and senior staff at his HQ at the former Raffles College in Bukit Timah. Here he told his men that they would have to obey the surrender instructions and keep the peace. That night, more than 300 Officers and men killed themselves by falling on their swords in the Raffles hotel after a farewell Saki party, and later an entire Japanese platoon killed itself using grenades. About 200 Japanese decided to join the Communist Guerrillas operating in Singapore.

When the liberation force arrived in Singapore, they could see for themselves the devastation and the emaciated state of the prisoners. They learned of the brutality and murder caused by the Japanese during their occupation of Singapore and beyond. One of the forces learned of the murder of his brother at the massacre of Alexandra Hospital and took his revenge on the surrendered Japanese. Cases like this were rife.

It was a few weeks before trucks would roll into the camps along the Death Railway to liberate the POWs. From his last camp, dad's friend Flash was put in the back of an open truck with other prisoners en route to Bangkok. Along the journey, he spotted a Japanese officer whom he recognised as one of the cruel, sadistic officers in one of the camps along the railway where he was interned. He screamed for the driver to stop and, with the screech of brakes, he jumped off the back of the truck, as weak as he

84

was, to confront this officer. This story was told to me by Flash and his wonderful wife, Neta, on one of our many meetings together.

The Japanese officer just kept bowing to Flash. Nobody on the truck, including FEPOWs, or those that liberated them, interfered. In fact, there was complete silence when Flash told the officer to remove his knee length boots. After doing so, Flash put these boots on himself and continued to kick this officer to death. From that day forth, he and his wife slept in single beds because every night of his life until he died, he kicked out in his sleep as he was reliving the day he killed the Japanese officer. Many men took their revenge along this journey, including the Chinese, who witnessed thousands of their countrymen beheaded at the fall of Singapore. It was also noted by witnesses that the Australians had a field day meting out punishment to their captors.

The liberation forces were sick to the stomach seeing the state of the men and some found it very difficult not to retaliate, with many turning a blind eye to what was going on towards the Japanese and Koreans. Who could blame them? A Man once said, "Forgive them for they know not what they do". Far for me to go against the word of our Lord, but after listening to Dad and other FEPOWs, I believe to this day that the Japanese and Koreans knew exactly what they were doing and never felt any remorse whatsoever for what they did.

When the trucks drove into Dad's camp, a young 18-year-old private, standing at the back of one of the trucks, shouted out, "Anyone from Camberwell (South East London)?" and my father shouted back, "Here son!". The young private, not knowing my father was a Colour Sergeant (not that it would have made a lot of difference anyway), said, "Ok mate, I'll look after you" and he gave my father a small piece of chocolate which he automatically spewed up. It was too rich for his stomach, a third of it anyway, as the other two-thirds were removed in his operation. True to his word, this young private took care of my father for the rest of the journey to Bangkok.

As the trucks from the camps made their way down to the Thai capital, another mate of my father's overheard two Australians, who had just spotted a Japanese guard by the side of the road on his knees looking up to the sky; one said to the other, "Ay mate, what do you think he is doing? Praying for forgiveness?" the other replied, "F*****g good luck with that one!".

Bangkok to Rangoon - Yangon as it is known today - 831.9 km. RAF evacuate allied prisoners of war from Thailand.

RAF Douglas Dakotas transported the liberated prisoners of war to Rangoon, Burma from Don Muang airfield near Bangkok, the capital of Japanese occupied Thailand. With warm beds, the best medical care and food awaiting them in Rangoon, one of the first airplanes out of Bangkok crashed killing all on board, included a Great Yarmouth lad from the Royal Norfolk Regiment. How tragic. It was devastating that these men had gone through three and a half years of hell on earth to come through all of that and be taken this way. Those that did arrive safely, including Dad, disembarked at Rangoon, boarded ambulances to hospital, and found themselves in the hands of the amazing hospital staff who were going to care for them.

In the grounds of the hospital, the POWs sat at garden tables with white tablecloths enjoying the newspapers and some, doubtless, long-missed tea and cigarettes served by British women. A time to drink tea, to take photos. The food for the men was heavenly, and their bodies soon responded to treatment. After various medical tests, many were given the all-clear and for them, the waiting to return home to Blighty began. For many others, the healing of their bodies would take longer. Some European and Australian POWs admitted to hospital suffered from blindness as a result of malnutrition. The precise reason was uncertain, but there was some improvement after the treatment by injection of crude liver extract. Since the surrender of Singapore, the men had never received any mail from back home and, worrying about the fate of their loved ones, the men put pen to paper and expressed exactly how they were feeling. So began their letters home. While recuperating in Rangoon hospital, the men got word that Lord and Lady Mountbatten were making a visit to the hospital. In honour of his visit my father led a parade of prisoners of war.

The next time the two would meet was in 1978 when Lord Louis Mountbatten visited my father at his home on the Isle of Wight.

14: Homecoming

On arrival at Rangoon hospital, the average weight of the POWs was approximately 6 stone, and some were in a worse state of health than others. They were completely broken men. Their state of health would determine how long their stay in hospital would be. When it was my father's time to return home, he left a few mates behind.

After recuperating in Rangoon hospital, Dad set sail on October 1st 1945 on SS Chitral (P&O) bound for Southampton.

Dad with Arthur Barker RAOC at Port Suez, in September 1945, on their way home

He was coming home.

The hardships that they all went through were not over for some of the men. On this journey back home, they received their back-mail that had been sent to them over three and a half years as prisoners of war. As Dad opened his first letter, a huge smile appeared on his face. Unbeknown to my mother at the time of writing this letter, my father had, of course, been captured at the fall of Singapore. It read:

"My dear John, I hope that wherever you are that you are safe and well. The girls and myself are off to a party tonight."

It was heartening to know that the family back home was well and to some extent enjoying life. Some of the other men's letters did not contain such innocent and pleasing words.

It is impossible to comprehend the resilience of the men to get through all that the Japanese threw at them. It is a testament to them - the true strength of their yearning for survival and the thought of returning home to their wives, mothers, families that kept the men going. My father taught me, as I'm sure others taught their children, that the mind is the most powerful thing in the world, and the body can take almost anything that is thrown at it. His thoughts were always to get through the torture, pain, and illnesses to return home to my mother and his son, my brother Terry. He, like many other prisoners, lost mates throughout those years as slave labourers to the Japanese.

Before the men received their back-mail, somewhere between leaving Rangoon on the Chitral to Southampton, they began to unwind, relax, and even enjoy their freedom. It was when the men received their correspondence that the atmosphere changed dramatically among some of them. Opening a letter from a member of their family declaring that their wives and children had died in an air raid bombing, or, indeed, their whole family had been killed, was to have a devastating impact, naturally. Others received news that their wives had run off with another man, believing that their husband had been killed in battle. These letters were often more than the men could bear.

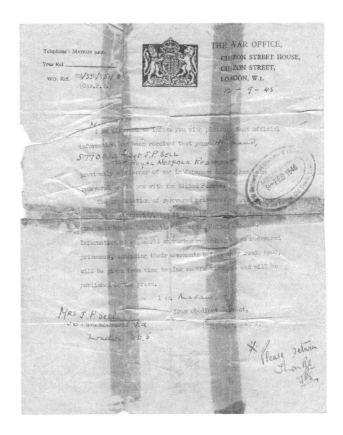

The only thing that had kept most of them going was the thought of returning home to their loved ones and this now had been tragically denied them. The first suicide was brought to my father's attention when he was informed that one of the men, having received such a letter, jumped overboard to his death. More and more suicides were reported when the men returned home, and psychological problems were to have a devastating impact on many of them, sometimes resulting in their death.

When my father arrived at Southampton on October 28th, there was none of the pomp and pageantry of a few months earlier on VE day. In fact, there was nothing like it! To many people the war had finished back in May 1945 and the celebrations were over. VJ Day (Victory in Japan) was practically forgotten then, much like it has been practically forgotten now.

"Here's your rail ticket home Sergeant and good luck" were the last words spoken to him when leaving Southampton for London.

My cousin, Francis, who was eight years of age, recalls my grandfather and my mother decorating the house with all the regalia they could lay their hands on. The only house in the street that was decorated, yet five months earlier the whole street had been alive with flags stretching from house to house, accompanied by a terrific street party. Throughout his incarceration, Dad managed to keep and hide two photographs from the Japanese. One was of my mother and brother, the other of Francis, his only niece at that time, which he returned to her when she got married. Francis also recalls watching her uncle - my father - walking down the street, Linnell Road in Camberwell, with another soldier. The other man was one of the unfortunates who had lost all his family during the bombings. My grandmother looked after him until he got well and was able to look after himself. On learning this, I asked Dad what had happened to him, but he didn't answer - just one more thing locked away in his thoughts.

The unsung forgotten heroes.

Mothers, wives, sweethearts, and family members. The ones that were told not to ask their sons, husbands, sweethearts, uncles, and brothers any questions of their time as a Japanese prisoner of war. The ones that had to try and rebuild the lives of their loved ones.

Broken men who had gone through hell on earth were going to return home as normal men. Not quite. The pain they suffered wasn't going to go away that easily. Men that were also told not to speak about their experiences as FEPOWs. Why were they told not to talk about it? To have to bottle up all that emotion, not to have anybody to speak to. My mother told me of a letter that she received stating that my father, on returning home, may act strangely but to let him be and eventually he will get better.

Today the illness is known as PTSD - post traumatic stress disorder. PTSD is an anxiety disorder caused by very stressful, frightening, or distressing events. People with PTSD often relive the traumatic event through nightmares and flashbacks, and may experience feelings of isolation, irritability, and guilt. Not many that returned home escaped suffering from PTSD and in some cases, they were much worse. My father's first night home was accompanied by a terrible nightmare - while thrashing about in bed, he got his head trapped in the metal bedstead and my mother called out to my grandfather to help her release him. But to no avail. They had to call the fire brigade who, on arrival, couldn't hold back their amusement. When my grandfather explained that Dad was a Japanese prisoner of war who had only returned home the previous day, they showed the utmost respect to him and released him as quickly as they could.

The hardest thing for Dad was being reunited with his son, Terry (my brother) whom he had not seen for over four years. When Mum introduced Terry to his dad, he would have nothing to do with him. He was afraid of him and kept asking her, "Who is this man? I don't like him". While Dad was away, my grandparents helped Mum raise Terry. That was all he knew until a 'strange' man entered his life and turned it upside down. My mother said this was a very difficult time for them all and that it took a long while for father and son to bond.

The pain, the misery, the beatings, the starvation, and the death/murders they all had witnessed, the beatings that my father had suffered and watched others suffer the same fate, was to have an almighty impact on the entire family. To survive all of this and then return home where his child didn't even know who he was just added to the pain. My mother helped Dad with the bonding process with Terry, who grew up to have the utmost respect for his father, following him into the Royal Norfolks when he was called up for National Service in the 50s. Such was the respect that he had for Dad, that when Terry sadly died in 2008, he was buried, at his request, with his dad in a cemetery on the Isle of Wight.

Every morning at exactly 3 am Dad would wake, get dressed, and walk the streets of London. Mum would wait for him to return home safely. Sometimes these episodes could last up to three hours. She was always there, never asking him where he had been. In fact, there were never any questions asked. It was only in later life that he began to open up and the subject could be discussed. Throughout his life, he always awoke at 3 am to visit the toilet (you could set your watch by him). I never found out the significance as to why 3 am meant so much to him, but clearly something happened that would have an enormous psychological impact on him for the rest of his life. When I learned of this through Mum, one evening while we were alone, I asked him, "Why dad? Why did you wake at 3 am every morning and walk the streets?" He replied, "Son, because I could".

On his return home he became a very heavy drinker. He was never violent but could be very cutting with his words towards my mother. Those early years were certainly not easy for her. As some might have said in those days, 'men were men and women were grateful.' The wives especially and, indeed, the families in general put up with a lot from the men on their return. But they saw it through, stood by them, even though they didn't quite understand why they were behaving in such a way. Mood swings, nightmares, and very poor health - how could they express themselves when told not to talk about their experiences as FEPOWs and the families told not to ask any questions? One person he did open up to and tell of his time as a FEPOW was a fellow Royal Norfolk, Percy Norman. They had joined up together in 1929. Percy had served with the 2nd Battalion and was captured by the Germans in France in 1940, then held at Stalag Camp number 383, Honenfels, in Bavaria. When hearing of Dad's time in captivity under the Japanese, he could not comprehend any of it. He had spent five years as a German POW and was treated with respect and given three square meals daily. Percy told me, as a young man, in comparison to my father's captivity, his was like a holiday camp.

In the years following his release, Dad attended Queen Mary's hospital in Roehampton, Richmond. Growing up as a young boy in the 1950s, I didn't know anything about my father being a FEPOW, I only remember him having to attend hospital on several occasions and not knowing why, just asking Mum if Dad was poorly.

Queen Mary's Hospital, Roehampton, Richmond.

In a group of 4,684 ex-FEPOWs released in 1945, 679 were found to have neurological disease - Optic Atrophy and Peripheral Neuropathy were of the most common. However, in at least 89 patients neurological disease developed many years after their release. 35 of these patients had cord lesions (spinal), not unlike those seen with multiple sclerosis, due to the condition of the camps along the Death Railway, and other recognised diseases. In addition, Parkinson's disease often developed many years after release with a prevalence much higher than that in the normal population. The experiences that these men had while in the Far East made them liable to develop cord disease and Parkinson's many years later.

Medical consequences of war attract little attention. The health consequences of the POW experience are still poorly researched or appreciated. The imprisonment of allied troop personnel by the Japanese during World War II provides an especially cruel story in terms of deprivation, malnutrition, and exposure to tropical diseases. Nutritional deficiency syndromes, dysentery, malaria, tropical ulcers, and cholera were just some of the major health problems ex-FEPOWs faced. There have been limited mortality studies on FEPOWs since repatriation, but these suggest an early (up to 10 years post release) excess mortality due to TB, suicides, and cirrhosis (likely related to hepatitis B exposure during imprisonment).

In terms of morbidity, the commonest has been a psychiatric syndrome, which would now be recognised as PTSD. This was present in at least one-third of FEPOWs and frequently presented itself decades later. Life in the hellish camps never left these men. Peptic ulceration, Osteoarthritis and hearing impairment also appear to occur more frequently, and in addition, certain tropical diseases have persisted in these survivors - notably infections with the nematode worm, strong yloides stercoralis - studies 30 years or more after release have shown overall infection rates of 15%. On my father's death certificate in April 1979, 34 years after release, it reads heart failure, unknown tropical diseases (worm found in bloodstream).

The Liverpool School of Tropical Medicine, established in 1898, was the first institution in the world dedicated to research and teaching in tropical medicine. Many men returned home from the Far East having contracted unknown tropical diseases. This term was used by medical specialists working at the Liverpool school. It took many years of research before they had any answers or, indeed, treatments for these tropical infestations.

My mother and father on their way to watch 'Gone with the Wind' at the Elephant and Castle, SE London, 1946

On my father's return from the Far East, on his first visit to Queen Mary's Hospital, after a thorough examination by a resident consultant, it was determined that he was suffering from an infestation of tapeworm/taeniasis, alongside malnutrition, dysentery, malaria and tropical ulcers. His symptoms included severe weight loss, nausea, general lethargy, abdominal pain and diarrhoea.

You must remember that these men had suffered appalling conditions for three and a half years, with a diet of less than 500 calories a day. As a result of this they would eat anything that they could lay their hands on.

78% of FEPOWs were diagnosed with some sort of infestation post-war. My father received treatment to cure the tapeworm over a period of seven years.

Our fathers suffered mentally and physically all their lives while the powers at that time were exonerated - 90% of those that were guilty of some of World War II's most horrendous crimes against mankind. I feel guilty on two accounts. Firstly, I have left it until now to write this book, so long after my father's death and, secondly, that I didn't fight decades ago for the answers that I want now.

Growing up from a boy to a young man alongside my father certainly holds many memories for me. As a boy, it was a strict upbringing, as a young man it was a pint or two down the local. One of my fondest memories was attending the annual COFEPOW (Children Of Far Eastern Prisoners Of War) Christmas parties held in Westminster Central Hall in the 1950s and early 1960s. This was one of the highlights of the year for us children. I recall sitting at long bench-like tables, watching magicians and clowns, and receiving a present at the end of the party. This also gave my father the opportunity to catch up with fellow FEPOWs. Every Christmas morning our phone would ring at approximately 11 o'clock and I would watch my father stand there, phone to ear, not saying a word, just listening until at the end he would speak his Christmas messages and replace the phone. It always baffled me until, as a young man, I got to learn the meaning of this phone call. It was from his mate, Flash. Flash sang the song 'Trees' to my father, originally sung by Paul Robeson in 1939. 'Trees' is a lyrical poem.

I think I shall never see a poem as lovely as a tree
A tree whose hungry mouth is pressed against the earth's sweet flowing breast

A tree that looks at God all day
And lifts her leafy arms to pray
A tree that may in summer wear a nest of robins in her hair
Upon whose bosom snow has lain
Who intimately lives in rain

What significance it held I am not quite sure.

Our strict upbringing was all about learning manners and respect, which I had in abundance for my Dad. Mealtimes as a child were all about manners. If you didn't eat all that was on your plate, then you didn't get any sweet. Naturally, he could not bear any food going to waste. Little did he know back then that Mum had already dished up the dessert, waiting for Dad to leave the room before serving it to us. If you wanted to leave the table, you had to ask permission, your knife and fork placed side by side, no laughing or joking about. Many a time my youngest sister, Barbara, would pinch me under the table, and we both got sent up to our rooms without finishing our meal. Fortunately, mum would come to the rescue again bringing us the remainder of our dinner. None of this ever did us any harm.

Sport played a major part in our family, Dad being a keen amateur cricketer and regimental boxing champion, and Mum an excellent runner, we were practically brought up on sport. My father took me just once to watch a football match. I was about 10 years of age when he took me to watch Millwall play. He could not abide any form of bad language, especially in front of women so I can count on one hand how many times I heard him swear. We were surrounded by, arguably, the most unruly football supporters in England and they didn't hold back on the expletives. We only lasted until half time when my father made excuses that we had to go home. From that moment on, he introduced us to cricket and boxing. Boxing, like any other contact sport, is all about discipline, when to retaliate and when to hold back.

I will never forget, as a young teenager, my mother bringing home matching kitchen appliances - a kettle and a toaster - that she got on the cheap (they fell off the back of a lorry). She had to remove the brand name of both appliances as they were manufactured in Japan. Nothing, and I mean nothing, was allowed in the house that was made by the Japanese. My mother thought she had got away with hiding the fact, until one evening when Dad was in the kitchen, Mum and I in the lounge, we heard the crash of two items being thrown out of the kitchen window. My mother hurriedly looked at me and whispered, "Don't say a word". Dad came into the lounge, sat in his chair without looking at my mother, and said, "I guess we'll be needing a new kettle" and never spoke for the rest of the evening. God only knows what the neighbours must have thought - Mrs Sell burnt Mr Sell's toast and made his tea too strong.

This was a turning point for me. I began to understand and realise the hurt and pain and, indeed, hatred he felt towards the Japanese. Hate is a strong word that, somewhat surprisingly perhaps, some FEPOWs did not approve of due to religious reasons and beliefs, and I must respect them for this. However, a high percentage of FEPOWs that I was fortunate enough to have met, held the same feelings towards the Japanese as my father held. In fact, some said the word 'hate' was not strong enough. Such were the strength of feelings they carried inside after years of enemy barbarism. Dad belonged to three FEPOW associations, obviously the Norfolk Association, the London Association of FEPOWS, and, on retiring to the Isle of Wight, the South and West Somerset FEPOW Club. These were all part of the National Federation of Far Eastern Prisoner of War Clubs and Associations of Great Britain and Northern Ireland (NFFCA)

I first heard the names Hintok, Three Pagodas Pass, Kanchanaburi, Chungkai, when fellow FEPOWs from different regiments visited our home in East Dulwich, South East London. Whenever they came to visit, Dad led them to the lounge and we were told to either go out to play or to be very quiet. While they talked on many occasions, I was lucky enough to earwig at the lounge door. These names of camps along the Death Railway meant nothing to me (I couldn't even pronounce Kanchanaburi) but for some reason that I can't explain, these names stuck with me.

It wasn't until Dad and I, a few years later, had our first talk together that I mentioned these names, wanting to know the meaning of them. He was dumbfounded to know where I had heard these names. I could never lie to my father, so I confessed that I earwigged and heard parts of his conversations. Even though he was displeased with me, he couldn't believe that I remembered the names of these camps after so many years. Still not grasping the true extent of his experiences as a FEPOW, and the memories he carried until the day he died, the relationship I had with him was growing stronger.

I would never purposefully hurt him, but one evening I played what I thought at the time was just a joke that completely backfired on me and would haunt me for many years. I was 17, had been out with my mates on a really cold night, and when I returned home, I walked into the lounge leaving the door open (no central heating in those days so the only warm room was the lounge). Mum and Dad were sitting in their chairs when my father told me to close the door as it was getting draughty. But before I closed it, I told him that I had brought a girl home.

"Well, bring her in son and introduce her."

Now that I had their full attention, I told them that I had something to tell them both.

"You haven't put her in the family way have you?"

"No dad, it's worse than that, she's Japanese."

My father sprang to his feet telling my mum to show the ***** the door. When I told him that I was only joking, he looked at me and told me very quietly to go to my room. He did not speak to me for three days. It completely tore me apart. How could I have been so stupid as to hurt him? I was completely thoughtless. This was the last time I ever played any kind of joke on him. It wasn't until after he died that Mum told me that on that night, he was initially extremely cross and was going to let me suffer in silence for those few days to teach me a lesson. It worked. As I look back at my childhood, I recall Dad took me to join the Boy Scouts, and I would also accompany him to the hairdresser. It wasn't until I got older that I knew I was in good hands. The Scout Master, Mr Scott as I knew him, and Doug the hairdresser, were both ex-FEPOWs who always made a fuss of me. I would hate to think I earned more badges as a Scout than the others because of my father's influence.

Evidence of War Crimes

15: Japanese War Crimes

War crimes were committed by the empire of Japan in many Asian pacific countries during the period of Japanese imperialism, primarily during World War II. These incidents have been described as an Asian holocaust. Most Japanese war crimes were committed during the part of the Showa era, the name given to the reign of Emperor Hirohito, until the surrender of Japan in 1945. The war crimes involved the Imperial Japanese Army and Navy under Hirohito and were responsible for the deaths of millions.

Historical estimates of the number of deaths which resulted from Japanese war crimes is 14 million through massacre, human experimentation, starvation and forced labour. Very few Japanese soldiers have admitted to committing these crimes. Airmen and Navy personnel were not included as war criminals because, apparently, there was no positive or specific customary international 'humanitarian law' that prohibited the unlawful conduct of aerial warfare. Yet the Japanese Army Air Service conducted chemical and biological attacks on enemy nationals.

Since the 1950s, senior Japanese government officials have issued numerous apologies for their country's war crimes. Japanese Ministry of Foreign Affairs states that the country acknowledges its role in causing "tremendous damage and suffering" during World War II. Members of the Liberal Democratic Party still deny some of the atrocities, such as government involvement in abducting women to serve as comfort women. Allied authorities found that Koreans and Taiwanese serving in the forces of the Empire of Japan also committed war crimes.

The Kempeitai

The Kempeitai, Military Police Corps, was the military police arm of the Imperial Japanese Army (IJA) from 1881 to 1945. It was both a conventional military police force and a secret police force, similar to the Nazi Gestapo only, arguably, worse. Most people are familiar with the feared Gestapo, the secret police of the Nazi regime, but their acts of terror and repression were more than matched by their Japanese counterparts, the Kempeitai. Founded in 1881 as the military police of the modernising IJA, they were largely unremarkable until the rise of expansionist Japanese imperialism after World War I. The Kempeitai became a brutal weapon of the state, holding jurisdiction over the occupied territories, captured prisoners of war and subject peoples. The Kempeitai worked as both spies and counter-intelligence agents. They used torture and extra-judicial execution to maintain their power over millions of innocent people.

When Japan surrendered, many documents were deliberately destroyed by the Kempeitai, so the true scale of their atrocities may never be known. After the Japanese occupied the Dutch East Indies, a group of about 200 British servicemen found themselves stuck in Java during the invasion. They took to the hills to fight as a gorilla resistance force but were captured and tortured by the

Kempeitai. According to over 60 eye-witness testimonies at the Hague following the war, these men were forced into one-metre-long bamboo cages meant to transport pigs. They were transported by trucks and open rail cars to the coast in temperatures reaching 38° degrees Celsius (100° degrees Fahrenheit).

The prisoners, already suffering from severe dehydration, were then placed on waiting boats, which sailed off the coast of Surabaya, and the cages were thrown into the ocean. The prisoners were drowned or eaten alive by sharks. The cruelty of the Japanese soldiers did not stop with the prisoners and, for fun, they caught stray dogs and placed them in bamboo cages, poured petrol over the poor dogs and set them on fire whilst standing around laughing, watching, and listening to these animals scream in agony. Another story told to me was of a captured monkey that the guards tied up outside their hut, stubbing out their cigarettes as they left. The screams of the monkey could be heard throughout the camp.

Those who were suspected of operating or building a radio, or smuggling medicine into the camps, were tortured by the Kempeitai. They were known to burn the flesh with cigarette lighters or drive metal tacks into their nails. One victim later described the Kempeitai's methods.

"The interviewer produced a small piece of wood like a meat skewer, pushed it into my left ear and tapped it in with a small hammer. I think I fainted sometime after it went through the ear drum. I remember the last excruciating pain and I must have gone out for some time because I was revived with a bucket of water. Eventually it healed, but, of course, I couldn't hear properly and have never been able to since."

Despite the crackdown, one Australian soldier, Captain LC Matthews, was able to organise an underground intelligence ring smuggling medical supplies, food, and money to prisoners, and to maintain radio contact with the Allies. He refused to reveal the names of those who helped him despite being arrested and tortured. He was executed by the Kempeitai in 1944.

Japanese actions in Singapore and Sandakan

After the Japanese captured Singapore, they renamed the city, Syonan (Light of the South) and set the clocks to Tokyo time. They then initiated a programme to clear the city of Chinese whom they considered dangerous or undesirable. Every Chinese male between the ages of 15 and 50 was ordered to report to registration points throughout the island for screening, where they would be closely questioned to determine their loyalties and political inclinations. Those who passed the tests were stamped on their faces, arms or clothing with the word 'examined'. Those who failed the tests - communists, nationalists, secret society members, English speakers, civil servants, teachers, veterans, and criminals - were taken to holding areas. For many, simply having a decorative tattoo was enough to be branded as a member of an anti-Japanese society.

For two weeks after the screening, those marked as undesirable were taken to be executed at plantations or coastal areas like Changi Beach, Ponggol Foreshore, and Tanah Merah Besar Beach, where their bodies would be washed out to sea. Methods of execution varied according to the whims of four section commanders. Some were marched into the sea and then machine gunned, while others were tied together before being shot, bayoneted, or decapitated (as they were in their thousands in Singapore). At later war crime trials, the Japanese claimed that there were around 5,000 victims. As we know from the records, the true figure is closer to 50,000. Following the massacre, the Kempeitai maintained a rule of terror and torture, including a form of punishment in which a victim was forced to ingest water by fire hose and then kicked in the stomach. One administrator, Shinozaki Mamoru, was so horrified by the torture that he issued thousands of "good citizen" and "safe passage" passes, usually intended only for those collaborating with the Japanese. He issued almost 30,000 of them, saving many Chinese lives, much to the fury of the Kempeitai. He is remembered today as "Singapore's Schindler".

The occupation of Borneo gave the Japanese access to valuable oil fields, which they decided to protect with a military airfield at the port of Sandakan using slave labour provided by prisoners of war. About 1,500 POWs, mostly Australians captured in the fall of Singapore, were sent to Sandakan where they endured horrible conditions with meagre rations of minimal vegetables and some dirty rice. They were later joined by British POWs in early 1943. The POWs were forced to labour on an airstrip while suffering from starvation, tropical ulcers, and malnutrition.

Some early escapes led to a crackdown at the camp. POWs were beaten, or imprisoned in open air cages in the sun, for crimes such as collecting coconuts or failing to bow deeply enough to a passing camp guard. In January 1945, the Allies bombed the Sandakan Air Base and the Japanese decided to withdraw inland to Ranau. Three death marches occurred between January and May. The first wave consisted of those considered most fit, who were loaded down with Japanese equipment and ammunition and forced to march through the tropical jungle for nine days with only four days of rations of rice, dried fish, and salt. Those left behind at Sandakan suffered malnutrition and abuse and were eventually marched south in two further waves. Those unable to move were left to die as the camp was torched during the Japanese withdrawal. Only six Australians survived the death marches.

A few Kempeitai of the East District Branch were sentenced to death after the war at the war crimes trials. One in particular, Kawamura Saburo, Commander of the Syonan (Singapore) Defence Garrison wrote in his memoirs, published in 1952 after his death, expressing condolences to the victims of Singapore and prayed for the repose of their souls. Five more were sentenced to life imprisonment to be served in Japan but only served five years until 1952 when Japan regained its sovereignty. They were therefore able to resume a normal life in society while our POWs carried the burden for the remainder of their lives. We can see why this would be a bitter pill for FEPOWs to swallow.

I guess the saying, "getting away with murder" rings true.

My personal views, based on my research, lead me to question "Did the mass-murderer Hirohito put his name to this? Did any form of life, other than their own, mean

112

anything to them?" The answer to this is no, pure and simple. How ironic it is that when Hirohito himself died on January 7th 1989, aged 87, he was buried wearing a Walt Disney Mickey Mouse watch. It is beyond belief for many, as is the fact that this man lived that long with this amount of blood on his hands. Sadly, it is too late to hold those accountable for his freedom.

Lieutenant-General Hitoshi Imamura, Commander-in-Chief of the Japanese forces in Java, was acquitted on war crimes charges by a court in the Netherlands, due to lack of evidence. However, he was later charged by an Australian military court and sentenced to 10 years in prison, which he served from 1946 to 1954 in Sugamo, Japan. To me, 8 years in a Japanese prison certainly suggests conspiracy. What about all the families of the men that were tortured and drowned? Didn't they mean anything? This man should have been hanged.

16: Evidence and the Trials for War Crimes

As a young teenager, before knowing the true extent of my father's experience as a FEPOW, I grew up with the knowledge of the Holocaust in Europe, the extermination of European Jews. I remember remarking about it to my father who just raised his eyebrows. It was when I was old enough, when my father and I sat down for many hours talking about his experiences, that I asked him why we had never been told of or taught anything about the atrocities committed by the Japanese army. Today, if you mention the word holocaust, people assume you are talking about what went on in Europe, not knowing anything of what went on in Asia. Unlike the Nazis, who were hunted all around the world and still are to this day, the Japanese military were exonerated for, arguably, the most heinous crimes in our history. Only a few were convicted for their crimes. Thousands went home to their family lives, while our men with continued with their personal battles for the rest of their lives. Our armed forces were clearly let down.

Not only were hundreds of Japanese war criminals exonerated for their crimes against humanity, but also there has never been enough said or done about their counterparts, the Koreans, recruited by the Japanese. In 1946 a British military court in Singapore tried a Korean national, Cho-Un-Kuk, for war crimes against allied prisoners of war on the Thai/Burma Death Railway during World War II. The evidence against Cho was scanty, but he had been part of a group of Korean guards notorious for brutality towards prisoners. In expedited proceedings relying heavily on affidavit material, Cho was found guilty and sentenced to 15 years in prison. The trial revealed both Cho's unexpected trans-national background as a dentist in pre-war British India and the complex position of Korean guards on the Death Railway.

Often characterised as universally brutal due to their own ill-treatment by the Japanese colonial system, the guards responded in many different ways to the pressures and opportunities of severe subordination to the Japanese military. After sentencing, Cho served time in both Singapore and Japan. He left prison, reportedly a 'broken man' in 1955 after only 9 years imprisonment (he was a broken man yet went on to live another 51 years until his death in 2006). Like other Koreans who had been in Japanese military employment. he was spurned by many of his countrymen as a collaborator. Only in 2006, after his death, was he officially recognised as an unwilling conscript into Japanese service (my question is - recognised by who?). His case illustrates the difficulty of distinguishing victims and perpetrators in the tangled circumstances of World War II.

Lee-Hak-Rae was a Korean youth who went to work at the age of 15, supervising prisoners of the Japanese who were mobilised to build the Thai/Burma Death Railway. Hintok, where he served, was the most dangerous place along the railway. Prisoners called it "Hell Fire Pass". Many Australians died there, mainly from overwork and diseases such as dysentery and cholera. Lee was indicted by an Australian court in Singapore on September 25th 1946, but on October 24th his case was dismissed in Hong Kong. En-route to Japan, he was then forced to return to

Singapore in March 1947 and was indicted for a second time.

The first of 3 charges lodged against Lee, whose Japanese name was Kakurai Hiromaru, was that he was neglectful of his duties in providing such things as food, medicine and clothing at the Hintok camp. Secondly, that he forced sick prisoners to go out on work details, and thirdly, he physically assaulted prisoners - exactly what was occurring in every camp along the Death Railway. On March 20th, Lee was condemned to death by hanging but 8 months later, on November 11th, his sentence was reduced to 20 years imprisonment. Why did they not hang him between these dates? Regarding the first charge, Lee's lawyer argued as follows: how could the lowest ranking civilian employee in the service of the Japanese army - a Gunzoku - be held accountable for the situation in a prisoner of war camp?

Abe Hiroshi, a platoon leader in the Japanese Railway Corps, said that even when officers of the Railway Corps requested medicines, they were not taken seriously. They were told that there was no reason to give anything to prisoners. Surely, if you deprive anybody of medicines to keep them alive, then that is tantamount to murder and you should, therefore, hang those responsible. Clearly a Gunzoku serving in the army had neither the authority nor the power to improve conditions. In addition, the prison camp took its orders from the Railway Corps and precedence was given to the construction orders of the imperial headquarters. The prison camp sent sick prisoners out to work.

The problem was this: did responsibility lay with the Railway Corps that requested prison labourers or with the authorities in the prison camp who forced them to go? The Railway Corps made the request, but the camp directly designated sick prisoners to work. Did the authority and responsibility for their dispatch rest with Lee-Hak-Rae? He argued that he had only sent prisoners out to work in accordance with orders. The third charge, beatings, Lee himself admitted. He said that he once struck an Australian prisoner who had violated regulations. The Japanese Army did not court martial violators of discipline but dealt with them by face slapping; beating their own without any cause was also an everyday occurrence within the Japanese army.

This way of thinking differentiated the Japanese and allied armies. Lee-Hak-Rae, whose training included being beaten, had a very shallow awareness of war crimes and, therefore, had his sentence reduced. Lieutenant-Colonel Edward 'Weary' Dunlop, the Australian military doctor, who had bitterly confronted Lee at Hintok, said that hanging was too severe, but that he should be punished for having driven sick prisoners out to work - some of the men that Lee sent out to work never returned to camp. He sent them out to their death. I totally disagree with 'Weary' Dunlop on this occasion. Dunlop also said that he had "no feeling other than regret" for a person who, when he is suffering, takes it out on others by hitting them. Although Lee was one of the lowest ranking civilian employees in the Japanese army, prisoners believed he had the authority to compel work and he became an object of hatred.

The Japanese military drafted 240,000 Koreans to serve in the military and in subordinate capacities as

117

civilians. Of these, 148 were convicted as B/C-class war criminals and 23 were hanged. The two reports on the case of Lee-Hak-Rae and other Koreans, who served Japan in the building of the Death Railway, raise important issues of war responsibility, human rights, and the nature of the Japanese Imperial Army. These B- and C-class War Crimes Tribunals, which unfolded concurrently with the Tokyo Trials, resulted in the conviction of thousands of low-ranking Japanese soldiers and civilian personnel who were in direct interaction with allied POWs. Korean personal also faced charges by their former prisoners, while the high command, for the most part, was left untouched. Many of those with least authority served long prison sentences.

Survivors of the Death Railway say that Korean and Taiwanese guards were the worst tormentors of allied prisoners and all should have been punished for their crimes. They also expressed their disgust at a campaign by a group of auxiliary troops from Korea and Taiwan, who were convicted of war crimes, to have their names cleared and to receive compensation. Thousands of these men served alongside the Japanese army in roles such as guards at Japan's notorious, brutal POW camps. 26 Taiwanese guards, as well as the 23 Korean guards, were subsequently executed.

A group of these veterans set up a group named Doshinkai in 1955 to demand that the government apologise for forcing them to join the Japanese military and, therefore being convicted of war crimes. The group also sought compensation for their claim that it damaged their reputations. Lee-Hyok-Rae, the 89-year-old chairman of the group, told a meeting in Tokyo that the Japanese government must apologise soon, as time was running out for their veterans. "I want to ask that our honour be restored very soon." Lee said. He also complained that while former servicemen, convicted of war crimes, receive monthly pensions, non-Japanese nationals receive a smaller amount. He said it is a tough situation and it is continuing. Moreover, he asked for support.

From the 240,000 recruited by the Japanese, a total of 49 Korean and Taiwanese were hanged. How so many got away with being the most vicious abusers is beyond me. Every one of these auxiliary troops should have been severely punished and yet they wanted to be honoured and compensated. What you need to remember is that these men volunteered and, presumably, knew exactly what they were doing. They mistreated the prisoners because they wanted to please their masters and were aware that they could get away with it. They joined up because Japan was winning the war and took advantage of that for their own gain and enjoyment. Many atrocities that they committed, including murders, executions, beatings, and sadistic torture, were in line with their Japanese superiors, so why did so many get away with these atrocities?

Will we ever get to know the truth?

17: Unit 731 (Caution: there are some distressing scenes described in this section)

Details in this section are taken from public records, evidence to War Crimes tribunals, and from a wide range of reference sources.

Known as Unit 731, Nana-San-Ichi-Butai was a covert biological and chemical research and development unit of the Imperial Japanese Army (IJA) that undertook lethal human experimentation.

I want to give you an insight into what my father and all the FEPOWs were about to face after the fall of Singapore. I hear most of you saying to yourselves that you have never heard of Unit 731. Sure, you have heard of the Holocaust, the murder of the 6 million Jews, the Jewish genocide cruelly committed by the Nazis of Germany and the monstrous experiments carried out by the likes of Dr Mengele, the 'Angel of Death' in Auschwitz, Birkenau and many other horrific concentration and death camps. However, this awful atrocity was not taught to us in school when I was a youngster, we had to learn about the Nazi Holocaust later in life through the media - television, film, and books.

Without wanting to undermine one of humanity's greatest crimes against itself, it does leave me with this begging question though. Why did we not know anything about the Japanese atrocities and, especially, Unit 731? This is one of the major subjects in this book and one that I will return to repeatedly. Without wanting to sound patronising, I would like to enlighten those whose knowledge is limited as to the sheer brutality of the Japanese during World War II.

This part of my story begins with the sadistic, barbaric brutality of the Japanese and their absolute lack of regard for human life.

The Japanese invasion of Manchuria began on September 18ᵗʰ 1931 with the aim of protecting Japan's interests in the railroad and the Kwantung leased territory. It was not until 1937 that the Japanese provoked the Chinese into full scale war. In 1935 the IJA set up Unit 731 in Pingfang Harpin led by Lieutenant-General Shiro Ishii, Medical Officer and Chief Microbiologist. This had the full backing of Emperor Hirohito, who knew what was to take place there. Such was the importance of this facility, they gathered 3000 of Japan's 'cream of the crop' scientists and medical staff to carry out heinous crimes against humanity, using state-of-the-art equipment.

Once the Unit was complete, it did not take them long to round up the first 'guinea pigs' for their experiments, consisting mainly of Chinese villagers and Russian workers caught up in the overthrow of Manchuria. The Japanese called these poor people 'logs', the sort one would toss on a fire. Incomprehensibly, human life did not appear to mean anything to them, and so they began experimenting on these 'logs' (the last time I use this sickening term). Human targets were used to test grenades, positioned at various distances and in different positions. The prisoners were tied down on boards, roughly the same size as an ordinary door, placed around in a circle and then a grenade was either placed or thrown into the centre of the boards. Once exploded, the staff would examine the 'outcome' on the prisoners. Some would have had their heads and limbs blown off, while others would be covered in shrapnel.

The ones that died were the lucky ones, for the survivors were subjected to other experiments - thousands of men, women and children interned at prisoner of war camps were subjected to vivisection without anaesthesia, which usually ended with the death of these poor victims. Vivisections were performed on prisoners after infecting them with various diseases. Researchers carried out massive invasive surgery on prisoners, removing organs to study the effects of disease on the human body. These were conducted while the patients were alive because it was thought that the death of the subject would affect the results.

Prisoners had limbs amputated in order to study blood loss. Limbs that were removed were sometimes reattached to the opposite side of the body. Some prisoners' limbs were frozen and amputated while others had limbs frozen, then thawed out, to study the effects of the resultant untreated gangrene and rotting. Other prisoners had their stomachs surgically removed and the oesophagus (tube that leads from the throat to the stomach) reattached to the intestines. Parts of the brain, lungs and liver were removed from some prisoners. An IJA army surgeon, Ken Yuasa, suggested that the practice of vivisection on human subjects, in this instance on Chinese communists, was widespread even outside Unit 731.

Prisoners were injected with diseases disguised as vaccinations to study their effects. To study the effects of

122

untreated venereal diseases, male and female prisoners were deliberately infected with syphilis and gonorrhea and then studied. Prisoners were also repeatedly subjected to rape by guards. Plague fleas infected clothing, and infected supplies encased in bombs were dropped on various targets in the region. The resulting cholera, anthrax and plague were estimated to have killed more than 400,000 Chinese civilians. Tularaemia is a severe, infectious bacterial disease of animals which was tested on innocent civilians. Once tested on humans, it resulted in extreme fever and weight loss.

Unit 731, and units established in other provinces, were responsible for the spraying of plague infested fleas, bred in the laboratories of Unit 731 and Unit 1644, and spread by low-flying aircraft on various Chinese cities. This military aerial bombardment killed thousands of people with bubonic plague. Physiologist, Yoshimura Hisato, conducted experiments by taking captives outside in perishingly cold weather, dipping their various appendages into water and allowing them to freeze. According to the testimony of a Japanese officer, the limbs were said to be frozen if, when struck with a short stick, they emitted the same sound as hitting a large board. Ice was chipped away, and the area doused in water. The effects of different water temperatures were tested by bludgeoning the victim to determine if any areas were still frozen.

Variations of these tests, in more gruesome forms, were performed by these men, who surely can only be described as evil. Some of these doctors orchestrated forced sex acts between infected and non-infected prisoners to transmit a disease, as stated in the testimony of a prison guard. Regarding the development of a method for transmission of syphilis between patients, the evidence states:

"Infection of the venereal disease by injection was abandoned and the researchers started forcing the prisoners into sexual acts with each other. Four or five Unit members handled the tests, dressed in white laboratory clothing that completely covered the body with only eyes and mouth visible. A male and female prisoner, one infected with syphilis, would be brought together into a cell and forced to have sex with each other - it was made clear to them that if they resisted, they would be shot."

After these victims were infected, they were vivisected at different stages of infection, without anaesthesia, so that internal and external organs could be observed as the disease progressed. Testimonies from multiple guards blamed the female victims as being hosts of the diseases even though they were forcibly infected. Genitals of female prisoners that were contaminated with syphilis were called 'jam filled buns' by guards. Some children grew up inside the walls of Unit 731 infected with syphilis. A youth core member deployed to train at Unit 731 recalled viewing a batch of subjects that would undergo syphilis testing.

"One was a Chinese woman holding an infant, one was a white Russian woman with a daughter of four or five years of age, and the last was a white Russian woman with a boy of about six or seven. The children of these women were also vivisected awake to determine how long the infection in different stages took hold."

Female prisoners were forced to become pregnant for use in experiments. The hypothetical possibility of vertical transmission of diseases, (from mother to foetus or child), particularly syphilis, was the stated reason for the torture. Foetal survival and damage to mothers' reproductive organs were objects of interest. Though a large number of babies were born in captivity, there have been no accounts of any survivors of Unit 731, children included. It is known (evidence statements) that all the children of female prisoners were murdered.

Men were subject to bacteriological, physiological, and sex experiments.

A former Japanese researcher recalled that one day, whilst waiting to perform a human experiment, there was still time to harm someone else. He and another Unit member took the keys of the cells and opened one that housed a Chinese woman and set about raping her. Immediately afterwards, the Unit member opened another cell. Inside this one there was a Chinese woman who had been used in a frostbite experiment. She had several fingers missing and her bones were black. Gangrene had set in, but he set about raping her anyway. Once he saw that her sex organ was festering, pus oozing to the surface, he gave up the idea and left.

What kind of man would even contemplate doing anything to this woman sexually?

It was a regular occurrence to test weapons on prisoners. Flamethrowers were used on them to see how long it took them to die. Human beings were tied to stakes as targets to test germ-releasing bombs and chemical weapons. In other experiments, these poor subjects were experimented on in different ways:

- deprived of food and water to determine the length of time until death
- placed into high-pressure chambers until they succumbed to death
- experimented upon to determine the relationship between temperature burns and human survival
- placed into centrifuges and spun until death
- injected with animal blood
- exposed to lethal doses of x-rays
- subjected to various chemical weapons inside gas chambers
- injected with seawater and burned or buried alive.

The 'scientists' of Unit 731 attest that most of the victims they experimented on were Chinese, while a small percentage were Soviet, Mongolian, Korean, and other allied POWs, including American and Australian. These researchers performed tests on prisoners using bubonic plague, cholera, smallpox, botulism, and other diseases. The Japanese planned to use plague as a biological weapon against San Diego, California. The plan was scheduled to launch on September 22nd 1945, but fortunately, Japan surrendered five weeks earlier.

Known Unit 731 members included Lieutenant-General Shiro Ishii; Lieutenant-Colonel Ryoichi Naito, founder of the pharmaceutical company, Green Cross; Masaji Kitano; Yoshio Shinozuka; Yasuji Kaneko.

18: War Crime Trials for biological warfare

With the advancement of the Red Army in August 1945, Unit 731 had to abandon its work in haste. Members of the Unit and their families fled to Japan. Ishii ordered every member of the group "to take the secrets of Unit 731 to the grave", threatening to find them if they failed and prohibiting any of them from going into public work back in Japan. Potassium cyanide vials were issued for use in the event that remaining personnel were captured. Skeleton crews of Ishii's IJA blew up the compound in the final days of the war to destroy evidence of their activities, but most were so well-constructed that they survived somewhat intact.

After the surrender of Japan, Lieutenant-Colonel Murrey Sanders, arrived in Yokohama. Sanders was a highly regarded microbiologist and a member of America's Military Centre for Biological Weapons. He was to investigate Japanese biological warfare activity. At the time of his arrival in Japan, he had no knowledge of what Unit 731 even was. Until Sanders threatened the Japanese with Soviet involvement, little information about biological warfare was being shared with the Americans. The Japanese wanted to avoid the Soviet legal system, so, the next morning after the threat, Sanders received the manuscript describing Japan's involvement in biological warfare. He immediately took this information to General Douglas MacArthur, who was the supreme commander of the allied powers, responsible for rebuilding Japan during the allied occupations.

This was the time when deals were made, when the regard for all those that suffered and died went out of the window. MacArthur struck a deal with Japanese informants. He secretly granted immunity to all the physicians of Unit 731, including their leader, in exchange for providing America with their research on biological warfare and data from human experimentation. American occupation authorities monitored the activities of former unit members, including reading and censoring their mail. The US believed that the research data was valuable. America did not want other nations, ironically the Soviet Union, to acquire any of this data on biological weapons. A crucial question is who is to blame here? Is it the Japanese for carrying out these terrible experiments on human life, or the Americans for covering it all up in the name of medical science? It would seem that both are equally to blame.

The Tokyo War Crimes Tribunal heard only one reference to Japanese experiments with "poisonous serum "on Chinese civilians. This took place in August 1946 and was instigated by David Sutton, assistant to the Chinese prosecutor. The Japanese defence counsel argued that the claim was vague and uncorroborated, and it was dismissed by the tribunal president, Sir William Webb, for lack of evidence. The subject was not pursued further by Sutton, who was possibly unaware of Unit 731's activities. Personally, given the evidence, I find it hard to believe that anyone, within a year of the war ending and working alongside the Chinese prosecutor, did not have a clue what the Japanese were involved in at Unit 731. His reference to it at the trial is believed to have been 'accidental'.

Clearly, human life, unimaginable suffering, and even death did not mean anything to anyone at this time.

Although publicly silent on the issue at the Tokyo trials, the Soviet Union pursued the case and prosecuted twelve top military leaders and scientists from Unit 731, its affiliated biological war prisons unit in Nanjing, Unit 1644, and Unit 100 in Changchun. During the Khabarovsk War Crime Trials, among those prosecuted for war crimes, including germ warfare, was General Otozo Yamada, the Commander-in-Chief of the million-man Kwangtung army occupying Manchuria. The trial of those captured Japanese perpetrators was held in Khabarovsk in December 1949.

A lengthy partial transcript of the trial proceedings was published in different languages the following year, via the Moscow foreign language press, including an English language addition. The lead prosecuting attorney at the Khabarovsk trial was Lev Smirnov, who had been one of the top Soviet prosecutors at the Nuremberg trials. The Japanese doctors (some of whom were responsible for handing out sweets laced with anthrax to Chinese children in villages around Unit 731) and army commanders who had perpetrated the Unit 731 experiments, received sentences from the Khabarovsk court ranging from 2 to 25 years in a Siberian labour camp.

The US refused to acknowledge these trials, branding them communist propaganda. The sentences doled out to the Japanese perpetrators were unusually lenient for Soviet standards, and all but one of the defendants returned to Japan by the 1950s. You can make up your own minds here. It was not long after this that the Soviet Union built

129

their own biological weapons facility, in Sverdlovsk, using documentation captured from Unit 731 in Manchuria.

Under American occupation, the members of Unit 731 and other experimental units were allowed to go free. One graduate of Unit 1644, Masami Kitaoka, continued to conduct experiments on unwilling Japanese subjects from 1947 to 1956 while working for Japan's National Institute of Health Sciences. He infected prisoners with rickettsia and mental health patients with typhus. All in the name of medical science.

After 40 years of one of World War II's closely kept secrets, Japan finally acknowledged what it had long denied. The Chinese to this day are still fighting for compensation. Each person associated with these units, along with Emperor Hirohito, should have been hanged for heinous crimes committed during World War II.

I believe that all those that gave these perpetrators immunity, in the name of medical science, namely Americans and Russians, should also have been prosecuted.

So, there you have it, an insight into the role of IJA and their views on human life during World War II.

19. Emperor Hirohito (referred to as the Mass Murderer by ex-FEPOWs) State visit to the UK.

Hirohito was known as The God among his people. His state visit to the UK was on October 5th 1971.

Her Majesty the Queen said at a dinner held for 170 guests that we cannot pretend the past did not exist. She went on to say that we cannot pretend that the relations between our two peoples have always been peaceful and friendly. However, it is precisely this experience which should make us all more determined never to let it happen again. Hirohito's reply made no reference to the past. He looked ahead to joint efforts with Queen and Country, for the preservation of tranquillity in the world, and the promotion of the welfare of mankind. The biggest stir arose when it was disclosed that Earl Louis Mountbatten of Burma, former supreme allied commander in South East Asia who accepted the Japanese surrender in 1945, would not attend the state banquet in honour of our FEPOWs. It was reported that he was so disgusted about the visit, that he snapped a Japanese ceremonial sword across his knee.

I remember my father also fuming in disgust over this visit. It was an absolute mockery, with no respect to those that died in captivity and to those that suffered for the rest of their lives. It was all to do with politics, trade between the two countries, the deals made behind closed doors when Japan surrendered in 1945. If Hitler did not commit suicide in his bunker would he have been exonerated for war crimes against humanity? We all know the answer to this - he would have been hanged. Two men considered to be mass murderers on a scale unlike any other, yet one lived scot-free into his late 80s.

Again, we have to question who was responsible for letting him live a normal life?

Referred to as a living god, he had a disciple (follower of God), General Tojo, nicknamed 'Razor' - an evil warlord who impressed Hirohito on his rise to power. So much so, that he placed Tojo as head of the infamous Kempeitai, who went on to orchestrate the horrors of Unit 731. Hirohito approved everything Tojo presented to him - he knew exactly what was going on. Even though reports suggested Hirohito was like a mushroom - 'keep him in the dark and feed him s***.' Tojo was fast becoming very powerful. Hirohito made him Minister of War and then Prime Minister. He held several posts and was highly regarded. However, the tide was turning for Japan and they were slowly losing their grip on the war.

The Americans were gaining ground in the Pacific, invading Saipan. On invading Saipan, they were horrified to witness mass suicide by the people of Saipan. Tojo persuaded Hirohito that the people of Saipan should commit suicide. 20,000 jumped to their deaths off the cliffs of Saipan, known today as 'Suicide Cliff'. In July of 1944, Tojo resigned, losing all respect from his erstwhile countryman and supporters. They blamed him for the downfall of Japan in the war. In 1946, Tojo called a doctor to mark the spot with a cross where his heart was so that he could commit suicide by shooting himself. The mark was there on his chest, so why did he shoot himself in the stomach? Gutless. Excuse the pun. Why did he not fall on his sword like most of his followers? On the December 23rd

1948, he was hanged. Yet some still believe Hirohito was innocent of war crimes.

Memories that never fade

20: Remembering their time in captivity

When the film *Bridge on the River Kwai* first appeared on our television screens, my father watched for about half an hour before saying, "Turn this s*** off". This was one of the few times I heard him swear. It wasn't until I got older, and watched the entire film, that I knew what he meant and why he got so upset watching it. We spoke about the film years later when he said it needed a writer to sit down with ex-FEPOWs and to listen to what they had to say. Only by hearing the truth would they be able to portray the truth. To this day, no film from that era has ever truly resembled the actual atrocities of the war.

In the early 1970s, my father and I sat down planning a road trip around Norfolk before he was due to retire from the Ministry of Defence, where he held the post of an EO (Executive Officer) in Whitehall, opposite Downing Street. The idea was for him to catch up with as many of his mates as he could before his retirement and planned move down to the Isle of Wight. As my father never drove, the designated driver was me and we were accompanied by my Mum and sister, Barbara. We set off early on Saturday morning - I'll call Dad the navigator and map-reader, as he sat next to me looking at a rather large AA road map.

Our first port of call was Kings Lynn, roughly 44 miles west of Norwich. Armed with just an address and not a very good navigator (no sat navs in those days!), the journey seemed to take forever before we reached our first destination. I cannot remember the guy's name, only that he was a sergeant in the 4th Battalion and a fellow FEPOW. His wife answered the door and showed us into the lounge, where he was seated by an open fire in the middle of summer. I will always remember that room as it was reminiscent of a museum dedicated to the Royal Norfolks. The curtains were drawn, and it was roasting hot, so clearly, this man was in poor health. He did not acknowledge me, my mother nor my sister, but beamed like a Cheshire cat when my father stood in front of him taking his hand.

I sat and listened to them talking, not about each other's experience at the hands of the Japanese, but how they were faring currently and whether they had maintained contact with any of their mates from the Norfolks. Occasionally, both would smile as they reminisced about someone from the regiment. The smiles didn't last long as they passed on information about the men they knew and what they were going through, i.e., ill health, separation from their wives and families due to their behaviour (the unlucky ones who couldn't cope with life in the aftermath of being FEPOWS). This was difficult listening for us as we sat there for what seemed like an eternity. Eventually, Dad stood up to say goodbye and his mate went to stand too, but my father placed a comforting hand on his shoulder and urged him to remain seated. A tear ran down the sergeant's face from his sunken eyes and I could see from my father's expression that this was going to be the last time they would ever see each other again. I thought about my Dad and how he would cope with all this emotion over the next two days. It was like he knew this was to be the last time he would see his mates and he

138

wanted to say his goodbyes to them all. When we returned to the car, there was an eerie silence amongst us, as if we didn't know what to say to each other. When he finally said, "O.K. son, Loddon next", the silence was broken.

So, we set off for the King's Head public house, Loddon in Norfolk, the home of proprietor, Sergeant Tommy Brown. It was prearranged between Tommy and Dad that this was to be our lodgings for the night. Witnessing the camaraderie between my father and his mates over the years certainly was to have a huge impact on me, especially when things turned sad. It played havoc with my emotions as I watched them hug and shed the occasional tear between them. This brought me back to the saying he once told me: "Son, all the while you have a hole in your backside, you will never experience true friendships like I have." Watching the closeness between Tommy and my father filled us all with immense pride.

That night in the pub, a few locals arrived and Tommy introduced them to my father explaining to them that he too was a Japanese prisoner of war. The fuss they made of him was incredible. They wouldn't leave him alone, wanting to know everything about his experiences as a FEPOW. The drinks were flowing, and my father was three parts to the wind when the door to the bar opened and in walked a man aided by his daughter, her arm interlocked with his. My father had his back to this gentleman, unaware that he was there. We noticed this man straighten up and then shout out, "All present and correct, Colour Sergeant." My father spun around seeing this man and his mouth dropped open. "Johnnie!" he exclaimed with his arms outstretched. The bar fell completely silent as my father held onto him, addressing him as, 'Nobby'. At this point my emotions got the better of me and I had to leave the bar for some fresh air. It wasn't my father's emotions I had to worry about, it was my own.

Once my composure returned, I came back to see three FEPOWs enjoying each other's company. The Japanese with all their atrocities - the malnutrition, starvation, beatings, and diseases - had not been able to stop these three men reuniting some 27 years after liberation! Tommy had arranged for Nobby Clark (all men with the surname Clark were called Nobby) to be at the pub knowing Nobby would not want to miss this reunion with my father. As this emotional night drew to a close Nobby declared and I quote, "I would not have missed this for the world." He turned around to me and exclaimed with immense pride, "You should have seen this man in the ring!" As we discovered that evening, Nobby was not a well man and it had taken a lot out of him just to be there. Bless him. After putting a very happy drunk father to bed, we all slept really well.

Royal Norfolks reunion, Gt Yarmouth. L-R, Flash Fuller, Dad, Tommy Brown, Jimmy O'Connor, Tom Power, unknown

The following morning, my father spoke with Tommy on the whereabouts of Jock Symonds, another mate from the 4th Battalion. Tommy explained to Dad that Jock was running a pub not too far away from Loddon. After we said our goodbyes and thanked Tommy for really looking after us and for his hospitality in general, we set off in search of Jock's pub. It was coming up to Sunday lunchtime before we finally found it - it was quite busy as it served Sunday lunch. My father was wearing his regimental tie (the Royal Norfolks). When we entered the pub, Jock was behind a very busy bar. My father stood behind my sister and I as I ordered the drinks with Jock, who turned towards the pumps and stopped dead in his tracks. He turned around and shouted, "Johnnie". Here again two mates who had not seen each other for years, hugging across the bar. The whole pub fell silent looking at the two men hugging. Again, I could not handle this and retreated outside. When the pub closed (2 pm back then) we left the two old soldiers to catch up on their past. On all our road trips together, this one was the most emotional - we hardly uttered two words together on our return journey home.

My brother David recalls that on one of the many evenings he spent with Dad in our local pub, one particular night a guy entered and approached them at the bar. Dad introduced him to my brother as Private Edward John Joyce, 2nd Battalion East Surrey Regiment -

Teddy Joyce, a fellow FEPOW. David noticed that all evening, Teddy never once put his hand in his pocket to buy a round of drinks. When David remarked on this to Dad, he replied that as long as he was alive and Teddy was in his company, he would never have to buy a drink. Then he explained why. He told David that when he was seriously ill, Teddy helped to save his life by bringing him extra food in the hospital hut. I can only presume this camp was Nakhon Pathom where Dad nearly lost his life.

In the late 60s, my brother Terry flew to the Far East to trace Dad's journey/route throughout Thailand. From Bangkok, he travelled up to Bang Pong to Thakanun, his last camp whilst working on the Death Railway before being sent down to Nakhon Pathom. Terry's guide took him to Chungkai and Kanchanaburi war cemeteries where he took photographs of all the men from the Royal Norfolk regiment - 4th, 5th, and 6th Battalions - that were buried there. Murdered by the Japanese army. He spent a day on the River Kwai, taking many photographs along the way of Wampo viaduct and the infamous bridge over the Kwai. He visited Hell Fire Pass and many other areas along the Death Railway where Dad was incarcerated. He put together as much information as he could at that time and returned home to England.

When he came round to Mum and Dad's house, we were all waiting to see what he had brought back from Thailand. He placed a bunch of photographs in my father's hand and, as he studied them, you could see the colour drain from his face. Dad was getting really upset. He passed the ones he had already looked at to my mother, who recognised many of the names on the burial plaques from her time spent in Gorlston before Dad was sent overseas. Some held more meaning than others. Watching Mum become upset along with my Dad was not pleasant - it was a long night in our household.

Terry asked Dad to join him on his next trip to Thailand. My father replied, "Why would I want to go back to that place, which holds my worst nightmares? The place where I witnessed the worst atrocities bestowed upon human beings you could ever imagine? The place where my mates were murdered? No, Son, I will not be joining you on any trip back there!"

It doesn't matter how you say it or describe it, it was murder.

If you die through starvation, then you have been starved to death. If you die through diseases, you have been deprived of life saving medicines and vitamins. If you die through the beatings and torture inflicted on you, then it is murder! You simply cannot describe it in any other way.

The honour in the end was theirs, the prisoners of war. Those that survived were never defeated by the Imperial Japanese Army. Even though they were a hardened force, they were weak of mind, showing themselves to be a sadistic cruel race who, I believe, would never have survived had the boot been on the other foot.

21: Memorabilia and Memories

On all the road trips and visits to FEPOWs I shared with my father – including Devon, the Isle of Wight, London, Suffolk, Manchester and, of course, Norfolk - it always amazed me how much Norfolk memorabilia these men had collected. There were regimental photographs, insignias, letters, and medals, framed on the walls of their lounges. This made me think, why didn't my Dad display anything of his time in the regiment? After all, he was a regular soldier with the 1st Battalion in India and then the 4th Battalion, total service time of 16 years 321 days. One of his prized possessions was the Kukri or Khukuri, a Gurkha fighting knife, that he had been presented with years earlier.

The Kukri or Khukuri is a knife originating from the Indian subcontinent, associated with the Nepali-speaking Gurkhas of Nepal and India. The knife has a distinct recurve in the blade. It is used as both a tool and a weapon on the Indian subcontinent. The two small knives that accompany the Kukri are the Karda and Chakmak, kept at the back of the sheath of the Kukri and used as a utility and, in an emergency, a sharpening knife.

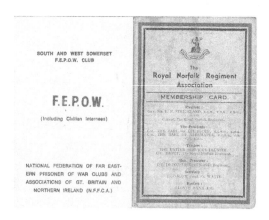

Dad treasured these, and they were put away for safety reasons. His regimental memorabilia was in a box at the bottom of the wardrobe, never on show, as if he did not want any reminders on display. He always wore his regimental tie and, on occasion, his blazer, which had the regiment's badge sown on it. He would wear this on our road trips and for his reunions. For years I never knew that he did not possess his war medals. It was only when we were watching the veterans march past the Cenotaph in London, all wearing their medals, that I asked Dad where his were. He didn't answer me and carried on watching the TV programme. It was one of those times when I knew not to continue with my questions, plus Mum looked over to me with her finger placed to her lips. It was later that evening, when Dad went to bed, that I got to learn about his medals. My Mum told me that when his medals arrived at his mother's house after the war, he told my grandmother to throw them in the bin. She asked him why, explaining that he had most definitely earned them.

146

"No, Mother, I did not earn any of these medals - they mean nothing to me."

Unbeknown to him, my grandmother never threw them away but kept them hidden until the day she died. We still do not know what happened to those medals after she passed away. I have never applied for copies of them. I feel that it would have been going against Dad's wishes.

Bert Read (Sherwood Foresters), South & West Somerset FEPOW Club, with dad on the Isle of Wight, 1977

On moving to the Isle of Wight in 1975, Dad soon became a member of the South and West Somerset FEPOW Club where he was visited on a few occasions by Bert Reid (Sherwood Foresters), a fellow FEPOW. I have no idea whether they knew each other on the Death Railway. This didn't seem to matter among FEPOWs, they all had one thing in common - they were prisoners of the Japanese for $3 \frac{1}{2}$ years, experiencing unimaginable cruelty and hardship.

We must never forget.

Tommy Brown visiting my father's grave on the Isle of Wight

It was in late 1977 that Dad's health started to deteriorate - shortness of breath and generally not feeling well in himself. With all his children living in and around London, the only communication we had with him was by telephone, speaking with Mum to enquire how he was. The answer was always the same: he was fine. They didn't want to worry us. And he was never going to let on to us just how poorly he was or how bad he was feeling.

22: Admiral of the Fleet - the Earl Mountbatten of Burma.

My Mum discovered, through Bert Reid, that Earl Louis Mountbatten was the Governor and Lord Lieutenant of the Isle of Wight. This gave her the idea to get in touch with Lord Louis' resident staff officer at County Hall, Newport, IoW, without my father knowing. Bert and my mother sat and composed a letter explaining all about Dad being a FEPOW, his failing health, and who happened to be living on the Isle of Wight. Another reason why Lord Louis would have sat up and taken notice of this request to visit my father, at his home, was because the last time the two had met was when Dad led a parade of able-bodied FEPOWs at Rangoon hospital in honour of Lord and Lady Mountbatten's visit before they set sail, back home to England. To Mum's surprise and happiness, she received a letter from Lord Louis' resident staff officer stating that Lord Louis would be more than pleased to visit my father and was looking forward to the visit. It was all arranged.

My sister Sandy, who at that time was a journalist on the British tabloid newspaper, the News of the World. She planned for a photographer and a reporter to attend and cover the story with all the local media, who somehow had got wind of two war veterans, mainly Lord Louis Mountbatten, meeting up after 30 years since their last meeting in Rangoon hospital. Dad was still oblivious to this meeting which took much planning by my mother. It was only two days before the event that she finally informed him of this illustrious visit - he was tremendously thrilled!

So, my brother David, sister Sandy, and I made our way from London to their home the day before the encounter. Even though Dad was not in good health, you would not have thought so on the actual day - he looked the happiest I had seen him for a while. All suited and wearing his regimental tie, I felt so proud him, he looked so dapper - like he always did every day working for the Ministry of Defence. A very smart man who did not suffer fools gladly. He always reminded me of two well-known English actors, David Niven, and Harry Andrews.

All the media had turned up at my parents' bungalow on Church Close, Wootton. Then we got word from the media that Lord Louis' cavalcade had pulled into the small estate. A chauffeur driven limousine, standard flying, and with a police motorcycle escort swept up to my parents' home. The first person to enter the bungalow was Lord Louis' equerry (an equerry is an officer of the British royal household who attends, or assists, members of the royal family in their official duties) firstly to see that everything was in order within their home and, secondly, to go through the itinerary with my father. Other than our parents, we were ushered into the kitchen until the meeting between Lord Louis and my father was over. It seemed like an eternity until we heard the equerry tell Lord Louis that they were running late for his next appointment. He swiftly replied, 'Let them wait."

When the meeting was over, Lord Louis added to my father, "Before I leave, I would like to meet your family." My parents then brought him into the kitchen where he was formally introduced to us. We shook his hand and his parting words have stayed with us forever.

"You have a very brave father."

Although we already knew this, it was a moment of immense pride to hear these words uttered by the great man himself. When the press had finished taking their photographs, Lord Louis was finally off to his next appointment having left a lasting impression on us all.

Dad returned to the bungalow having said his goodbyes, beaming like a Cheshire cat and said, "Well, he must have enjoyed himself because he stayed longer than he had planned." Little did my father know Lord Louis had had his staff research his life in the military (he didn't need a script). He knew when Dad joined up in 1929, he knew every camp in which my father had been interned along the Death Railway, and the parade at Rangoon hospital. Dad said he knew more about him than he knew himself!

*Admiral of the Fleet the Earl Mountbatten of Burma shakings hands
with my father, my mother in background, at home*

Lord Mountbatten with my father at his home 1978

GOVERNOR AND LORD LIEUTENANT OF THE ISLE OF WIGHT

ADMIRAL OF THE FLEET THE EARL MOUNTBATTEN OF BURMA

KG. PC. GCB. OM. GCSI. GCIE. GCVO. DSO. FRS

COUNTY HALL,
NEWPORT,
ISLE OF WIGHT,
PO30 1UD

2nd March 1979

My dear John Snell,

I have heard from your friend, Bert Read, that you
have not been at all well recently and as I am just off
on a trip abroad I thought I would write a little line
to wish you well.

As I told you when I came to visit you and your wife,
I do admire your courage in having risen above the horrible,
cruel treatment you received at the hands of the Japanese,
to have resumed at least a civilised existence.

I did enjoy visiting your delightful home and meeting
your charming wife.

I hope the doctors are looking after you properly and
if you need any further help while I am away you can always
write to my Resident Staff Officer, John Horsnell, Esq., at
County Hall, Newport.

Once more, all my best wishes.

your sincerely

Mountbatten of Burma

*Letter from Lord Mountbatten to my father on hearing news of his poor
health*

How ironic and deeply sad that both would die the following year.

Late in 1978, Dad's health was deteriorating and yet it didn't stop him weeding his garden on his backside - that was the kind of man he was. He would not let anything beat him. For a man of his years, and one who had lived through unimaginable horrors, he sailed through his illness until his body, quite simply, had had enough. This great, noble, and strong man had become bed bound.

Early in 1979, he was transferred by ambulance from his home on the Isle of Wight to the Queen Elizabeth

Military Hospital on Woolwich Common, South East London. This was an amazing hospital with the very best medical care we could have wished for. He was there for a while, receiving excellent medical attention, when Mum was called to attend a meeting with an RAMC (Royal Army Medical Corp) captain, my father's consultant. We all accompanied her to the hospital, then we were shown into a room where the doctor was waiting for us. In no uncertain terms, he told us that my father was dying. I could not get my head around this at all and refused to accept it. There was nothing more they could do for him, they said. He was transported back to the Isle of Wight to end his days in his own home.

In April of that year, I went down to spend some time and help Mum with my dad, still refusing to accept the inevitable. To me, he was just unwell but would come through it. The first thing he asked me to do was to set up the portable television in his bedroom so he could watch the cricket, which he loved, and, secondly, would I carry him to the bathroom so he could have a bath. I lifted him from the bed and the first thing I noticed was the weight loss. He weighed next to nothing. Being a very proud man like men of his generation were, when I removed his pyjamas, he tried to hide his dignity. We really laughed as I said, "Dad, you're gonna have to wash your privates yourself." That was the last laugh we would share together. At the end of the week, we hugged and kissed, and said our goodbyes. That was to be the last time I saw my father alive.

A week later he passed away, peacefully, on April 28th 1979.

GOVERNOR AND LORD LIEUTENANT OF THE ISLE OF WIGHT

ADMIRAL OF THE FLEET THE EARL MOUNTBATTEN OF BURMA
K.G., P.C., G.C.B., O.M., G.C.S.I., G.C.I.E., G.C.V.O., D.S.O., F.R.S.

COUNTY HALL,
NEWPORT,
ISLE OF WIGHT,
PO30 1UD

9th May 1973

Dear Mrs. Sell,

On my return from a visit to Germany I received the sad news that your brave and wonderful husband, John, passed away on the 28th April.

I hasten to send you my sincere condolences in this tragic loss.

I well remember visiting you both at your beautifully kept home and being very happy to have the chance of a good gossip with your late husband.   He had all the best qualities that a man could have to face up to the appalling time as a Japanese prisoner-of-war.

Having lost my own wife I can imagine only too well what you are going through now and you have my most sincere sympathy.

Yours sincerely,

Mountbatten of Burma

Letter from Lord Mountbatten to my mother after hearing of my father's death

I had lost my dad, my best friend, and my hero. As far as I was concerned, the Japanese had murdered my father. He was only 67 years of age but blessed for every year he lived. His dying wish was to be buried in a rice sack like many of his mates who died along the Death Railway. However, sadly, we were unable to fulfil his dying wish.

Sorry Dad!

He was buried in the cemetery of the Royal Church of St Mildred's, Whippingham, Isle of Wight, in the same grounds, somewhat ironically, as Lord Louis' parents, the Battenbergs. His dear friend, Flash, was a pallbearer along with my brothers, Terry, David, and me. He was also represented by members of the Royal Norfolk Regiment, one of whom was WO2 (Warrant Officer Class 2) George Johnson, who my father had served with in India with the 1st Battalion. George was not a FEPOW but had gone on to fight the Japanese in Imphal and Kohima throughout the war.

When Dad returned home from being a FEPOW, he was awarded a War Disability Pension of approximately 60%. They only raised it to 100% when they were informed by my mother that he was dying. It has only come to my attention in the last few years that not all prisoners were awarded a disability pension.

Why?!

Clearly, every one of them should have been in receipt of one. My Dad deserved his and it is a travesty that others were not as fortunate as he was, and were not given what should have been rightfully theirs!

My brother David on the bridge over the Kwai in 2016

23: Compensation for FEPOWs

It was many years, and following many battles, before there was any compensation paid for wrongs suffered by Britons held as POWs by the Japanese during WWII.

On November 7th 2000 the British government announced that, on a claim made to the War Pensions Agency, it was to make an ex-gratia payment of £10,000 to all surviving members of British groups held prisoners by the Japanese during World War II. Where a member did not survive to November 7th 2000, the surviving spouse was entitled to claim for the full amount. If the member survived to this date, but died before making a claim, either the estate or the surviving spouse was able to make the claim themselves. It is known as the Far Eastern Prisoners of War Ex-gratia Scheme. The survivors and widows of those who had since died were given this one-off payment in recognition of what the Defence Minister, Lewis Moonie, called their 'unique experience'. He said the tax-free ex-gratia payment would repay a debt of honour.

Then why did it take the Government 55 years to honour our fathers, and indeed, our mothers? Why mention 'tax free' as if they were doing our fathers a favour?

"Here you go lads, the Government is giving you £10,000, but don't worry it is all tax free!"

What an insult.

After all, surely it was the duty and responsibility of the British Government to all members of the armed forces, the merchant navy, and civilians, who had served their nation with honour and pride during the war years, to ensure that on their return home they would not have to wait many decades to receive this payment.

In the words of some, they were forgotten people.

16,700, together with more than 4,500 widows (including my mother, a widow, as Dad had passed away 21 years earlier) were to be paid by the Blackpool-based War Pensions Agency as soon as was possible.

There are still searching questions about why it took 33 years for the British Colonial Government in Malaya to pay out a total £1.5 million to the widows and dependents of Malayan residents, who, after all, had died building the Death Railway. Malaysia settled its overall claims with Japan in 1967, accepting several million dollars as reparations. Yet our fathers, who had been sent to the Far East only to become prisoners of the Japanese, had to wait 55 years before being considered for a payment of £10,000. Let down by successive British governments, as they have always been, the payment of £10,000 was a pittance. It should have been £10,000 for each year spent as a prisoner. What value do you place on those who died a horrible death, or those that returned home and suffered trauma for the rest of their days?

Every year, on my Dad's birthday, his first words were, "Who would have thought that I would have reached this age?" It was a blessing for him that he had done so after losing so many of his friends during incarceration, and so many more before he himself passed away.

My Mum received the compensation along with many other widows - and rightly so! As I have said before, they were the unsung heroes who deserved every penny.

161

They were the ones having to endure the trauma, and the stress, of looking after their men, which, in many cases, was certainly not easy for them. However, Dad never got to 'enjoy' this compensation and, to be perfectly honest, I don't know how he would have responded to it anyway. That said though, I am certain that if this payment had been paid out to all our brave fathers and mothers years earlier, it would have made a positive difference to their lives.

It all came too late!

Shame on you, the British Government, for letting all of them down.

Those in authority failed them as they still do to this day. As responsible children, it has been our duty to educate those that are still unaware of what went on in the Far East. We are constantly fighting the fight to keep our fathers' memories alive. Most of my Dad's grandchildren were born after his death, and those that were born before he passed away were far too young to know much of their grandfather's past.

Today though, they *all* know.

Some have shown more interest than others, including my youngest daughter, Cassie, who never got to meet her granddad. When she was old enough, she started to ask questions while studying photographs of her grandparents. She became more inquisitive about my father as she grew, to the point of becoming infatuated. She wanted to know everything about him.

Whilst living in Tenerife, purely by chance I met a young Dutch couple - Cassie and I were out shopping when we stopped at a very busy restaurant for lunch. We were shown to a table, which was the only one left, where this couple was sitting. We smiled and made pleasantries and ordered our lunch. The couple mentioned that they were going to Thailand. Before they could finish their sentence, my Cassie who was 14 years old at this time blurted out that her grandfather was a Japanese prisoner of war and had worked on the Death Railway. I sat looking at her in amazement looking before I could elaborate on what she had said. The young Dutch girl smiled and said, "So was my grandfather."

A light lunch suddenly became a long drawn out, but welcome, affair. I could not stop thinking what a small world we live in. There we were, in a restaurant, in Tenerife, sitting with a charming, young Dutch couple discussing the Death Railway. My Cassie was enthralled. It turned out the young girl's grandfather was a Dutch civilian internee, captured in Singapore. Her grandmother, along with many other women, fled aboard a ship from Kepple harbour. She told me that her grandfather had survived but her grandmother told her that he was not the same man who had kissed her goodbye that fateful day. When he finally returned home to the Netherlands, he was in very poor health and passed away at an early age. She was going to Thailand to discover as much information as she could about her beloved grandfather, as well as his friends who had died there. I wished them all the luck in the world as we were leaving. My only regret is that we never stayed in touch.

In 2003, we had to return to the UK, Great Yarmouth to be precise, on business. How ironic to return to the actual place where it all began. On the 11th of the

163

11th, Cassie and I attended the remembrance service at the memorial situated along Great Yarmouth's seafront. It was dedicated to the soldiers of the Royal Norfolk Regiment, who became prisoners of war of the Japanese after the fall of Singapore. To my utter surprise and delight, amongst the congregation, I recognised Jock Symonds, who I had not seen since the early 70s with my father. He did not recognise me or recall our meeting - that came as no surprise to me, as I spent most of the time outside his pub trying to pull myself together. The most important thing was, he remembered my father and, indeed, my mother, from the Gorleston days when she came to be with Dad before he was shipped to the Far East. This was when Jock told me the story of when he helped Dad with the distribution of sugar to the men in Changi. This was the last time I saw Jock alive.

Cassie was completely overwhelmed by this meeting, as well as meeting with other 'Norfolks', and she asked them if they knew her granddad. It was the start of our journey together - she has attended meetings with fellow COFEPOWs with me. Her knowledge of the Far East was growing and getting stronger all the time. Together we attended Norwich cathedral NFFWRA (National FEPOW Fellowship Welfare Remembrance Association) on Sunday February 12th 2017 to commemorate the 75th anniversary of the fall of Singapore. What I, with many other COFEPOWs from up and down the UK, observed while attending this service of remembrance was the lack of media coverage. It was practically non-existent, like it has always been. Not much of a surprise there then.

One of our annual visits is to a church in Wymondham, Norfolk. This church was built in 1952 by Fr ML Cowin, who, as a WWII FEPOW in Thailand, made a solemn vow to build a living memorial to all POWs who died in the prisons and internment camps of the Far East under Japanese control. The service takes place on the Sunday closest to the 14th May every year, the anniversary of the relief of Rangoon in 1945, so that it does not clash with other commemorations but is very appropriate. A very moving service, which always results in my Cassie crying. As we, the children of FEPOWs, grow older, we must continue to educate younger generations. This church stands as a sign that we will not forget.

We must never forget the debt of honour we owe! Our children and their children will hopefully continue the fight when we are gone. Those in authority failed them as they are still failing us. When will they get the recognition they truly deserve? Only time will tell.

Enough said.

In loving memory of my hero, Colour Sergeant Johnnie Sell, Royal Norfolk Regiment

Epitaph to a FEPOW

A FEPOW stood at Heavens door
His face was lined and thin
He softly asked St Peter
"Please may I come in?"
St Peter asked "What have you done. That you should
be admitted here?"
"I was a Japanese Prisoner of war
For almost three and half a years" The Pearly
Gates swung open
And St Peter rang the bell
"You've earned your place in Heaven 'cos you've had
your share of Hell"

To honour those who served their country

"In this their finest hour"

5770032

Colour Sergeant

John Percy Sell

1910/11/12 - Born Camberwell, London

Son of John and Dorothy Sell

1929/08/17 - Enlisted

1938 - Married Irene Derriman, in Camberwell District

Royal Norfolk Regiment

4th Battalion

1942/02/15 - Singapore Capitulated

1942/02/15 - WO 417/42, Missing

WO 417/61, previously posted missing now reported a PoW

WO 417/98, reported a PoW Malaya

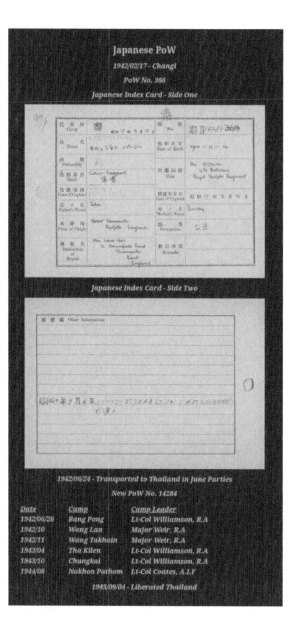

1942/06/24 - Transported to Thailand in June Parties

New PoW No. 14284

Date	Camp	Camp Leader
1942/06/26	Bang Pong	Lt-Col Williamson, R.A
1942/10	Wang Lan	Major Weir, R.A
1942/11	Wang Takhain	Major Weir, R.A
1943/04	Tha Kilen	Lt-Col Williamson, R.A
1943/10	Chungkai	Lt-Col Williamson, R.A
1944/08	Nakhon Pathom	Lt-Col Coates, A.I.F

1945/09/04 - Liberated Thailand

Appendices

Appendix 1: Camps along Burma Railway

- Nong Pla Duk (start of construction in June 1942 by British POWs from Singapore).
- Nong Pla Duk Junction.
- Ban Pong (transit camp and first P.O.W hospital).
- Ruk Khe.
- Tha Rua Noi (transit camp for prisoners marching North).
- Tha Muang (base camp for many workers).
- Kanchanaburi (Kanburi to the men, war cemetery) hospital camp.
- Khwae Yai Bridge.
- Bridge of the River Kwai.
- Khao Pun.
- Chungkai (war cemetery) main hospital camp, POW camp.
- Wang Lung. "LAN".
- Wang Yen.
- Thapong.
- Ban Khao (Dutch POWs discovered neolithic artefacts here).
- Thakilen.
- Lum Sum.
- Ai Hit.
- Tham Krasae Bridge.

- Wang Po (the Wampo viaduct).
- Wang Yai.
- Nam Tok.
- Nam Tok Sai Yok Hoi.
- Thasao (HQ and hospital).
- Thasao camp (transit camp for workers marching North).
- Tonchan (commenced work here on arrival from Singapore May 1943).
- Tampil (workers camp).
- Hell Fire Pass.
- Hintok (Weary Dunlop's camp, many deaths here from cholera).
- Kannyu (POWs from this camp worked on the infamous Hell Fire Pass).
- Sai Yok.
- Kinsaiyok (mixed nationalities, site of shooting British POW).
- Tamajao 237
- Tamajao 241
- Tamajao 239
- Lin Thin (Dutch camp).
- Kuiyae (Dutch POWs killed in allied bombing 1944).
- Hindat.
- Prang Kasi (Dutch camp).
- Yongthi (Australian and Dutch camp).
- Thakanun.
- Nam Chon Yai.

- Tha Mayo (Indian workers occupied this camp during construction).
- Tamrong Patho.
- Kroeng Krai (six Australians killed in a rock fall).
- Kurikonta.
- Konkoita (Australian camp, 7 Japanese and Koreans from this camp were hanged for crimes).
- Thimongtha.
- Shimo Ni Thea;
- Ni Thea.
- Sonkrai (Australian camp of 400 men, suffered many deaths).
- Chaunggahiaya (British camp, 214 died here, buried in a single mass grave).
- Paya Thanzu Tuang (this camp situated just North of 3 Pagodas Pass).
- Aungganaung (a work camp, later used as a grouping camp).
- Regue;
- Kyondaw (transit camp, many died here).
- Lawa.
- Apalon Bridge (site of one of the seven steel railway bridges).
- Apalon.
- Apalaine (base hospital).
- Mezali (in a filthy condition).
- Kami Mezali.
- Lonsi.

- Tanngzun (dead Asians found in huts, start of Cholera epidemic).
- Thanbaya Camp.
- Thanbaya (desperately sick brought here from Thailand, 700 died in less than 6 months).
- Anankwin.
- Myettaw.
- Beketaung (184 Americans arrived here October 1942).
- Tanyin (Number 1 mobile force).
- Retphaw (became base hospital after repeated bombings at Thambyuzayat).
- Konnoki.
- Rabao.
- Thetkaw.
- Wagale (Dutch camp).
- Sin-Thanbyuzayat.
- Thanbuyuzayat (War cemetery) base hospital camp.

Appendix 2: **The Rules of The Bushido Code**

Bushido was, and for many still is, the code of ethics and behaviour of the legendary Japanese Samurai warriors.

The seven virtues that define Bushido are as follows:

- Jin: Benevolence towards mankind; universal love; compassion.

- Makoto: Utter sincerity; truthfulness.

- Chugi: Devotion and loyalty.

- Meno: Honour and glory.

- Yu: Valour; bravery; heroism.

- Rei: Proper behaviour; courtesy.

- Gi: The right decision, taken with equanimity; rectitude.

To the thousands of Jap soldiers that strongly believed these virtues, and to those that committed suicide after Japan surrendered because of their beliefs, it is beyond me that those that survive forgave their God, Emperor Hirohito for surrendering Japan. After all, death to them was an honour. Hypocrisy comes to mind here. He let his country down and his followers of Bushido. It is my belief that he should have committed the

Japanese ritual of suicide by disembowelment, known as hari-kari.

Index

Duke Sell

Duke was born 1952 in East Dulwich, South-East London and educated at Thomas Carlton Secondary School.

He spent a number of years living abroad, working as a promoter of entertainment and the arts, and had his own 8 page newspaper pull-out covering all aspects of entertainment.

He has also put together a variety of live shows, mainly 'An Audience With', including with such famous sportsmen as Frank Bruno, Jackie Charlton and many more.

He met his wife Lynne 40y ears ago and they have two daughters Emma and Cassandra. He lives in Maidstone, Kent.

Printed in Great Britain
by Amazon